Keto Queen: The Ultimate Guide to Ketogenic Living for Women

DNT Publishing

Published by DNT Publishing, 2024.

KETO QUEEN: THE ULTIMATE GUIDE TO KETOGENIC LIVING FOR WOMEN

First edition. February 7, 2024.

Copyright © 2024 DNT Publishing.

ISBN: 979-8224801114

Written by DNT Publishing.

Table of Contents

Introduction: Nourishing Women through Ketogenic Living

Welcome to "Nourishing Women through Ketogenic Living," a comprehensive guide crafted specifically to address the unique needs and considerations of women on their journey into the world of ketogenic living. This book is your key to unlocking the transformative power of the ketogenic diet, tailored to meet the distinct physiological and hormonal aspects that women experience.

1.1 Understanding Ketogenic Diet

In this introductory section, we delve into the historical roots and evolution of the ketogenic diet. Gain insights into the science behind ketosis, exploring the metabolic changes that occur within the body. We'll lay the foundation for your understanding of ketones, their impact on brain function, and the myriad benefits that women can derive from embracing this lifestyle.

1.2 Benefits of Ketogenic Living for Women

Embark on a journey to discover the manifold advantages of adopting a ketogenic lifestyle tailored for women. From weight management and fat loss to the intricate balance of hormones crucial to women's health, this section sets the stage for the transformative possibilities that lie ahead.

2. Fundamentals of Ketogenic Diet

Dive deep into the core principles that make the ketogenic diet a powerful tool for women's well-being. Explore the science behind ketosis, unravel the mechanics of how the diet works on a cellular level, and gain insights into the nutritional components that form the bedrock of ketogenic living.

3. Getting Started

The path to success begins with a thoughtful and personalized approach. Assess your health, define your goals, and navigate the initial challenges as you transition into the ketogenic lifestyle. This section provides practical advice on setting realistic expectations and forging a path that aligns with your unique journey.

4. Customizing Ketogenic Diet for Women

Acknowledge the distinct nutritional needs of women as we guide you through the art of customizing the ketogenic diet. Delve into the nuances of adjusting macronutrient ratios, considering the role of protein and fat in achieving optimal health. Special attention is given to the impact of the ketogenic diet on hormonal health, from menstrual cycles to pregnancy and beyond.

5. Meal Planning and Recipes

Crafting balanced and delicious meals is an art, and this section serves as your culinary guide. Explore the intricacies of meal planning, sample meal plans tailored for women, and a treasure trove of flavorful ketogenic recipes that cater to diverse tastes and preferences.

Understanding Ketogenic Diet: Unraveling the Science and Principles

Welcome to the foundational chapter of "Nourishing Women through Ketogenic Living." In this section, we embark on a journey to unravel the science and principles that underpin the ketogenic diet, shedding light on its historical context, evolution, and the intricate metabolic changes it induces within the body.

Origins and Historical Context

Explore the origins of the ketogenic diet, tracing its roots from historical practices to its modern application. Discover how the diet, initially developed for medical purposes, has evolved into a lifestyle choice embraced by many for its transformative health benefits.

Evolution of Ketogenic Diet for Women

As we delve into the evolution of the ketogenic diet, a special focus is placed on its adaptation to suit the unique needs of women. Uncover the journey of how this dietary approach has been tailored to address the physiological and hormonal intricacies that distinguish women's health.

Benefits of Ketogenic Living for Women

Having laid the historical groundwork, we turn our attention to the practical implications of adopting a ketogenic lifestyle. Explore the multitude of benefits specifically tailored to women, ranging from effective weight management to the intricate balance of hormones crucial for overall well-being.

Weight Management and Fat Loss

Discover how the ketogenic diet becomes a powerful ally in the pursuit of weight management and fat loss for women. Delve into the science of ketosis and understand how the body's reliance on fat for energy can lead to sustainable and healthy weight outcomes.

Hormonal Balance and Women's Health

This subsection explores the intimate connection between the ketogenic diet and hormonal balance in women. From menstrual cycles to pregnancy and menopause, grasp how ketosis can positively impact hormonal health, offering a holistic approach to well-being.

Origins and Historical Context: Tracing the Roots of Ketogenic Wisdom

Embark on a historical voyage through the origins and context that birthed the ketogenic diet, a nutritional approach with roots deeply embedded in both ancient practices and medical history.

Primitive Echoes of Ketosis:

The concept of ketosis finds echoes in early human dietary patterns. Investigate how ancestral diets, characterized by periods of food scarcity and reliance on fats, inadvertently led to the metabolic state known as ketosis. We'll explore the innate capacity of the human body to adapt to diverse nutritional landscapes.

Medical Genesis:

Transitioning to the modern era, witness the medical genesis of the ketogenic diet. Trace its inception as a therapeutic intervention in the early 20th century, designed to manage epilepsy in children. Uncover the pioneering work of medical professionals like Dr. Russell Wilder and how they laid the groundwork for the diet's medical applications.

War, Fasting, and Epilepsy:

During World War II, scarcity of food resources prompted researchers to examine the effects of fasting on the human body. Delve into how these studies contributed to our understanding of ketosis and paved the way for the ketogenic diet's application beyond epilepsy management.

Evolution into a Lifestyle:

Witness the gradual evolution of the ketogenic diet from a medical intervention into a lifestyle choice. Explore pivotal moments where individuals, seeking not just therapeutic benefits but also overall health improvements, began adopting the ketogenic lifestyle. This transformation marked a shift from medical necessity to personal choice.

The 21st Century Resurgence:

In recent decades, witnessed the resurgence of interest in the ketogenic diet. Examine the role of technological advancements, increased scientific scrutiny, and a growing health-conscious community in catapulting the ketogenic diet into the mainstream. Explore the intersection of ancient wisdom and modern science that fuels the resurgence of this nutritional paradigm.

Evolution of Ketogenic Diet for Women: Tailoring Ketosis to Feminine Wellness

In this segment, we embark on a nuanced exploration of how the ketogenic diet has evolved to cater specifically to the unique needs and intricacies of women's health, reflecting a transformation from a generalized approach to a more personalized and gender-sensitive nutritional paradigm.

Foundations in General Ketogenic Principles:

Begin by revisiting the foundational principles of the ketogenic diet, and understanding its metabolic impact and benefits. Lay the groundwork for comprehending how these principles, initially developed for a broad audience, form the basis for later adaptations specific to women.

Recognition of Women's Distinct Physiology:

As awareness grew regarding the distinct physiological aspects of women's bodies, delve into how the ketogenic community recognized the need for tailored approaches. Explore pivotal moments where researchers and practitioners began to acknowledge that women's health requires a nuanced understanding, especially concerning hormonal fluctuations, reproductive stages, and unique nutritional needs.

Incorporating Hormonal Health into Ketogenic Living:

Witness the integration of hormonal health into the ketogenic lifestyle. Understand how the diet is adapted to consider the menstrual cycle, pregnancy, and menopausal transitions. Explore research and insights that have shaped the development of ketogenic protocols customized for women's hormonal well-being.

Pregnancy and Ketogenic Diet:

Navigate through the evolving perspectives on ketogenic living during pregnancy. Examine how the diet has been adapted to accommodate the needs of expectant mothers, addressing concerns related to fetal development, maternal health, and the dynamic hormonal shifts that occur during this critical period.

Fine-Tuning Macronutrient Ratios:

Explore the fine-tuning of macronutrient ratios specifically for women. Delve into the delicate balance of protein, fats, and carbohydrates, considering not only energy needs but also the impact on hormonal balance, muscle preservation, and overall well-being.

Addressing Women's Health Concerns:

Uncover how the ketogenic lifestyle has actively addressed common health concerns unique to women. From thyroid function to managing symptoms associated with menopause, witness the adaptability of the ketogenic diet to serve as a supportive nutritional framework for women at various life stages.

Benefits of Ketogenic Living for Women: Empowering Well-being Through Ketosis

This section unveils the manifold benefits awaiting women who embrace the ketogenic lifestyle, illustrating how ketosis becomes a transformative ally in enhancing both physical and hormonal well-being.

Weight Management and Fat Loss

Embark on a journey into the realm of effective weight management and sustainable fat loss. Understand how the ketogenic diet, through the metabolic state of ketosis, optimizes the body's utilization of stored fat for energy. Explore the nuances of fat loss specific to women, considering hormonal influences and the intricate balance necessary for achieving and maintaining a healthy weight.

Hormonal Balance and Women's Health

Delve into the profound impact of ketogenic living on hormonal balance, a cornerstone of women's health. Explore how ketosis positively influences hormonal regulation, offering potential benefits in managing menstrual cycles, fertility, and symptoms associated with menopause. Uncover the empowering role of the ketogenic lifestyle in nurturing overall hormonal harmony, contributing to a sense of well-being unique to women.

Holistic Approach to Women's Wellness:

Beyond weight and hormonal considerations, discover the holistic benefits of the ketogenic lifestyle. From improved mental clarity and enhanced energy levels to stabilized blood sugar levels, witness how ketosis contributes to a comprehensive approach to women's wellness. Explore the potential alleviation of symptoms related to conditions such as polycystic ovary syndrome (PCOS) and other hormonal imbalances.

Metabolic Flexibility and Endurance:

Uncover the concept of metabolic flexibility as a key benefit of ketogenic living. Understand how the ability to seamlessly transition between using carbohydrates and fats for energy empowers women with increased endurance, both mentally and physically. Explore how this adaptability supports sustained energy levels throughout various activities and life stages.

Inflammation Reduction and Longevity:

Dive into the anti-inflammatory effects of the ketogenic diet, exploring how it may contribute to the reduction of inflammation—a factor linked to numerous chronic health conditions. Investigate the potential implications of a ketogenic lifestyle for promoting longevity and optimizing the aging process, offering women a pathway to vibrant and resilient health.

Weight Management and Fat Loss: Navigating the Ketogenic Path to a Healthy Body

In this section, we delve into the intricate relationship between the ketogenic lifestyle and effective weight management, exploring how ketosis becomes a powerful tool for sustainable fat loss, with a specific focus on the nuances relevant to women.

Metabolic Symphony of Ketosis:

Embark on a journey into the metabolic symphony orchestrated by ketosis. Understand how the ketogenic diet induces a state where the body shifts its primary energy source from carbohydrates to fats. Dive into the science behind ketosis and its impact on metabolism, paving the way for effective weight management.

Fats as Fuel for Weight Loss:

Explore the paradigm shift in viewing fats as a primary fuel source for weight loss. Uncover how the body, in ketosis, taps into stored fat reserves, offering a sustainable and efficient mechanism for shedding excess weight. Delve into the intricacies of fat utilization and the benefits it brings to women seeking a healthier body composition.

Hormonal Considerations for Women:

Recognize the unique hormonal considerations that women navigate on their weight loss journey through ketosis. Understand the role of estrogen, progesterone, and other hormones in shaping the body's response to the ketogenic diet. Explore how hormonal balance becomes a key factor in achieving and maintaining weight loss goals.

Balancing Act: Hormones and Caloric Deficit:

Navigate the delicate balancing act of achieving a caloric deficit for weight loss while considering hormonal equilibrium. Explore strategies to create a sustainable and balanced approach to calorie management, ensuring that weight loss goals are met without compromising women's hormonal health.

Practical Tips and Strategies:

Equip yourself with practical tips and strategies tailored for women pursuing weight management and fat loss through the ketogenic lifestyle. From meal planning to mindful eating practices, discover actionable steps that enhance the effectiveness of the ketogenic approach while fostering a positive relationship with food.

Long-Term Maintenance and Sustainability:

Peer into the long-term horizon of weight management and sustainability within the ketogenic lifestyle. Understand how ketosis offers not just initial weight loss but a sustainable pathway to maintaining healthy body composition. Explore lifestyle adjustments and habits that contribute to the lasting success of weight management goals.

Hormonal Balance and Women's Health: Orchestrating Well-being through Ketosis

In this section, we unravel the intricate relationship between hormonal balance and women's health within the context of the ketogenic lifestyle. Discover how ketosis becomes a guiding force, fostering equilibrium and vitality in the realm of hormones.

Harmony in Hormonal Regulation:

Embark on a journey into the profound impact of the ketogenic lifestyle on hormonal regulation. Uncover the delicate dance between hormones and well-being, as ketosis influences key players such as insulin, cortisol, and sex hormones. Explore the science behind how the ketogenic diet contributes to a harmonious hormonal symphony.

Menstrual Cycles and Hormonal Fluctuations:

Navigate the nuanced landscape of menstrual cycles and hormonal fluctuations in the context of ketogenic living. Understand how ketosis can potentially impact the regularity and symptoms associated with menstrual cycles. Explore the scientific evidence and real-world experiences shedding light on the intersection of hormonal health and the ketogenic lifestyle.

Fertility and Reproductive Health:

Delve into the relationship between the ketogenic diet and fertility, exploring how hormonal balance plays a pivotal role in reproductive health. Uncover insights into the potential benefits of ketosis for women planning for pregnancy, addressing conditions such as polycystic ovary syndrome (PCOS), and supporting overall reproductive wellness.

Menopausal Transition:

Explore how the ketogenic lifestyle becomes a supportive ally during the menopausal transition. Understand the hormonal shifts that accompany menopause and discover how ketosis may offer relief from symptoms such as hot flashes, mood swings, and changes in metabolism. Gain practical insights into navigating this transformative life stage with resilience and vitality.

Thyroid Function and Ketogenic Living:

Peer into the interplay between thyroid function and the ketogenic lifestyle. Understand how ketosis may influence thyroid hormones and explore considerations for women with thyroid conditions. Uncover practical strategies for maintaining thyroid health while reaping the benefits of the ketogenic approach.

Holistic Wellness and Hormonal Harmony:

Expand your perspective to view hormonal balance as a cornerstone of holistic wellness. Explore how the ketogenic lifestyle goes beyond addressing specific hormonal concerns, contributing to overall mental clarity, emotional well-being, and vitality. Witness the transformative potential of hormonal harmony as it radiates through various facets of women's health.

Fundamentals of Ketogenic Diet: Navigating the Science and Principles

Welcome to the core of "Nourishing Women through Ketogenic Living." In this section, we embark on a comprehensive exploration of the fundamentals that constitute the bedrock of the ketogenic diet. Gain insights into the science behind ketosis, understand how the diet works on a physiological level, and explore the essential nutritional components that define the ketogenic lifestyle.

Science Behind Ketosis:

Embark on a journey into the intricate science behind ketosis, the metabolic state that defines the ketogenic diet. Unravel the mechanisms that lead the body to prioritize the utilization of fats for energy. Explore the role of ketones in fueling the brain and how ketosis offers a unique metabolic advantage for those seeking transformative health outcomes.

How Ketogenic Diet Works:

Delve into the workings of the ketogenic diet on a physiological level. Understand how the dietary shift to high fat, moderate protein, and low carbohydrates triggers metabolic adaptations, leading to ketosis. Explore the impact of ketosis on insulin sensitivity, blood sugar levels, and the body's utilization of stored fat for energy.

Nutritional Components of Ketogenic Diet:

Navigate through the nutritional components that form the foundation of the ketogenic lifestyle. Explore the optimal ratios of macronutrients—fats, proteins, and carbohydrates—that characterize a well-formulated ketogenic diet. Understand the importance of micronutrients, vitamins, and minerals in ensuring a balanced and nourishing approach to ketogenic living.

Macronutrient Ratios:

Dive deeper into the nuanced world of macronutrient ratios within the ketogenic framework. Understand the ideal balance of fats, proteins, and carbohydrates that promotes and sustains ketosis. Explore practical strategies for customizing macronutrient ratios based on individual needs, goals, and metabolic considerations.

Micronutrient Considerations:

Examine the role of micronutrients in optimizing health within the ketogenic lifestyle. Explore the importance of vitamins, minerals, and other essential nutrients in supporting overall well-being. Gain insights into sourcing micronutrients from diverse food options to ensure a nutrient-dense and wholesome ketogenic approach.

Science Behind Ketosis: Unveiling the Metabolic Alchemy

In this section, we delve into the intricate science behind ketosis—the metabolic state that distinguishes the ketogenic diet. Unravel the physiological processes that transform the body into a fat-burning powerhouse and explore the fascinating interplay of molecules that underpin this metabolic alchemy.

Energy Metabolism 101:

Embark on a journey through energy metabolism, understanding the body's default reliance on glucose derived from carbohydrates. Explore how ketosis redefines this paradigm, shifting the primary fuel source to fats. Gain insights into the metabolic flexibility that ketosis offers, allowing the body to seamlessly transition between carbohydrates and fats for energy.

Ketone Bodies: The Metabolic Stars:

Enter the realm of ketone bodies—the metabolic stars of ketosis. Uncover the process of ketogenesis, where the liver synthesizes ketone bodies, namely beta-hydroxybutyrate, acetoacetate, and acetone. Explore the role of these molecules in providing an alternative, highly efficient energy source, especially for the brain.

Brain Fuel Switch:

Peer into the fascinating brain fuel switch that occurs during ketosis. Understand how ketones cross the blood-brain barrier to become the primary energy substrate for the brain. Delve into the cognitive benefits associated with this shift, including improved mental clarity, focus, and potentially neuroprotective effects.

Insulin Sensitivity and Blood Sugar Regulation:

Examine the impact of ketosis on insulin sensitivity and blood sugar regulation. Understand how the ketogenic diet can contribute to stabilizing blood glucose levels, making it a valuable approach for individuals with insulin resistance or type 2 diabetes. Explore the potential benefits of metabolic health and weight management.

Fat Adaptation and Lipolysis:

Navigate the process of fat adaptation—a hallmark of the ketogenic lifestyle. Explore how the body becomes adept at utilizing stored fat for energy through lipolysis. Understand the role of hormones, such as insulin and glucagon, in orchestrating this metabolic dance, leading to enhanced fat breakdown and utilization.

Physiological Indicators of Ketosis:

Discover the physiological indicators that confirm the presence of ketosis. Explore methods for measuring ketone levels, from urine strips to blood ketone meters. Gain practical insights into interpreting these indicators and fine-tuning the ketogenic approach to optimize individual metabolic responses.

Metabolic Changes During Ketosis: Unraveling the Body's Transformation

In this section, we embark on a detailed exploration of the metabolic changes that unfold within the body during ketosis—the transformative state at the heart of the ketogenic lifestyle. Uncover the intricate processes that redefine energy metabolism, influence hormone regulation, and contribute to the unique benefits associated with ketosis.

Shifting Energy Substrates:

Embark on a journey through the metabolic landscape as the body undergoes a profound shift in its choice of energy substrates. Explore how the transition to ketosis redirects the primary fuel source from glucose derived from carbohydrates to ketone bodies synthesized from fats. Understand the metabolic flexibility that emerges, allowing the body to seamlessly switch between these energy substrates.

Enhanced Fat Utilization:

Dive into the mechanics of enhanced fat utilization—a hallmark of metabolic changes during ketosis. Explore how the body becomes a highly efficient fat-burning machine through increased lipolysis and beta-oxidation. Uncover the role of ketones in providing a constant and sustainable energy source, especially for tissues like the brain and heart.

Insulin Sensitivity and Glucose Regulation:

Examine the impact of ketosis on insulin sensitivity and glucose regulation. Understand how reduced carbohydrate intake and reliance on ketones can contribute to improved insulin sensitivity. Explore the potential benefits for individuals with insulin resistance or metabolic disorders, leading to stabilized blood sugar levels and enhanced metabolic health.

Ketones as Brain Fuel:

Peer into the fascinating adaptation of the brain to utilize ketones as its primary fuel source. Delve into the science behind how ketones, particularly beta-hydroxybutyrate, cross the blood-brain barrier to fuel the energy-demanding organ. Explore the cognitive benefits associated with this metabolic shift, including heightened mental clarity and focus.

Elevated Ketone Levels:

Explore the factors influencing the elevation of ketone levels during ketosis. Understand how dietary choices, fasting, and individual metabolic responses contribute to the production of ketones. Gain insights into measuring and interpreting ketone levels using various methods, providing valuable feedback on the depth of ketosis.

Potential Benefits for Weight Management:

Navigate the potential benefits of metabolic changes during ketosis for weight management. Explore how enhanced fat utilization, appetite regulation, and hormonal balance can contribute to effective weight loss and maintenance. Understand the role of ketosis in promoting a favorable metabolic environment for those seeking transformative changes in body composition.

Ketones and Brain Function: The Cognitive Symphony of Ketosis

In this section, we unravel the fascinating interplay between ketones and brain function—the cognitive symphony that distinguishes the ketogenic lifestyle. Explore the profound impact of ketosis on the brain, uncover the neuroprotective effects, and understand how ketones become a preferred source of energy for optimal cognitive function.

Energy-Efficient Brain Fuel:

Embark on a journey into the realm of brain energy metabolism, understanding how ketones emerge as a highly efficient fuel source for the brain. Explore the metabolic advantages of ketones, including their ability to provide a constant and sustainable supply of energy, leading to improved cognitive performance and mental clarity.

Crossing the Blood-Brain Barrier:

Delve into the intricacies of ketones crossing the blood-brain barrier—a crucial step in their role as brain fuel. Explore how ketones, particularly beta-hydroxybutyrate, navigate this protective barrier to reach the brain's cells. Understand the significance of this process in ensuring a stable and reliable energy supply for optimal brain function.

Cognitive Benefits of Ketosis:

Uncover the cognitive benefits associated with ketosis. Explore how individuals in a state of ketosis often report heightened mental clarity, improved focus, and enhanced cognitive performance. Peer into research findings that suggest potential benefits for conditions such as neurodegenerative diseases and neurological disorders.

Neuroprotective Effects:

Navigate the neuroprotective effects of ketones, exploring their potential role in safeguarding the brain from oxidative stress, inflammation, and other factors linked to neurological decline. Delve into research insights suggesting that ketosis may have protective implications for conditions like Alzheimer's disease, Parkinson's disease, and epilepsy.

Hormonal Influence on Neurotransmitters:

Examine the hormonal influence of ketosis on neurotransmitters—chemical messengers that play a crucial role in brain communication. Understand how the ketogenic lifestyle can impact the production and balance of neurotransmitters such as dopamine, serotonin, and gamma-aminobutyric acid (GABA), contributing to mood regulation and cognitive well-being.

Adaptation and Cognitive Flexibility:

Explore the concept of cognitive flexibility—a key aspect of brain function influenced by ketosis. Understand how the ability to seamlessly switch between fuel sources enhances adaptability and resilience in cognitive tasks. Gain insights into real-world applications of cognitive flexibility and its implications for daily life.

How Ketogenic Diet Works: Unveiling the Metabolic Mechanics

In this section, we delve into the physiological intricacies of how the ketogenic diet works, uncovering the metabolic mechanics that distinguish it from conventional dietary approaches. Explore the transformative journey from dietary intake to ketosis and understand the key principles guiding the body's adaptation to this unique nutritional paradigm.

Dietary Shift to High Fat, Moderate Protein, Low Carbohydrates:

Embark on the foundational aspect of how the ketogenic diet works—the dietary shift. Explore the principles of consuming high amounts of healthy fats, moderate protein, and significantly reducing carbohydrate intake. Understand how this strategic alteration in macronutrient composition sets the stage for the body's metabolic transformation.

Inducing Ketosis:

Delve into the process of inducing ketosis—a metabolic state characterized by the production and utilization of ketone bodies for energy. Explore how the reduction in carbohydrates prompts the liver to produce ketones, specifically beta-hydroxybutyrate, acetoacetate, and acetone. Understand the role of ketones in fueling various tissues, especially the brain, during periods of low carbohydrate availability.

Impact on Insulin Sensitivity:

Examine the impact of the ketogenic diet on insulin sensitivity and blood sugar regulation. Understand how the reduction in carbohydrate intake leads to lower insulin levels, promoting improved insulin sensitivity. Explore the potential benefits for individuals with insulin resistance, type 2 diabetes, and metabolic disorders.

Metabolic Adaptation and Fat Utilization:

Navigate the process of metabolic adaptation as the body transitions to utilizing fats for energy. Explore enhanced fat breakdown through lipolysis and increased beta-oxidation. Understand how ketosis optimizes the body's ability to tap into stored fat reserves, providing a continuous and efficient source of energy.

Brain Adaptation and Ketone Utilization:

Uncover the brain's adaptation to ketone utilization—a key aspect of how the ketogenic diet works. Explore how ketones, particularly beta-hydroxybutyrate, serve as a preferred fuel source for the brain, crossing the blood-brain barrier. Understand the cognitive benefits associated with this shift, including improved mental clarity and focus.

Maintenance of Ketosis:

Explore strategies for maintaining ketosis within the ketogenic diet. From mindful food choices to monitoring macronutrient intake, gain insights into practical approaches that support the sustainability of ketosis. Understand the factors influencing individual metabolic responses and fine-tune dietary practices for optimal outcomes.

Impact on Insulin and Blood Sugar: Balancing Metabolic Harmony

In this section, we explore the profound impact of the ketogenic diet on insulin sensitivity and blood sugar regulation, uncovering the metabolic harmony achieved through strategic dietary choices.

Reducing Carbohydrate Intake and Insulin Levels:

Embark on the journey of how the ketogenic diet influences insulin levels through a reduction in carbohydrate intake. Explore the principle of minimizing the consumption of high-carbohydrate foods, leading to lower insulin secretion. Understand how this reduction in insulin levels contributes to improved insulin sensitivity.

Promoting Insulin Sensitivity:

Dive into the concept of insulin sensitivity—a crucial factor in metabolic health. Explore how the ketogenic diet promotes improved insulin sensitivity, allowing cells to efficiently respond to insulin signals. Understand the potential benefits for individuals with insulin resistance, metabolic disorders, and those seeking optimal blood sugar regulation.

Stabilizing Blood Sugar Levels:

Explore the role of the ketogenic diet in stabilizing blood sugar levels. Understand how the reduction in carbohydrates leads to fewer fluctuations in blood glucose, providing a more stable and controlled environment. Delve into the potential benefits for individuals with type 2 diabetes and those aiming for balanced energy levels throughout the day.

Reducing Glycemic Load and Impact:

Navigate the concept of glycemic load and its impact on blood sugar. Explore how the ketogenic diet, characterized by low glycemic load, minimizes spikes in blood glucose levels. Understand the implications for maintaining metabolic stability and avoiding the negative consequences associated with frequent blood sugar fluctuations.

Potential Benefits for Metabolic Disorders:

Examine the potential benefits of the ketogenic diet for individuals with metabolic disorders, such as insulin resistance and type 2 diabetes. Understand how the strategic manipulation of macronutrients positively influences insulin sensitivity, leading to better blood sugar control. Explore the implications for long-term metabolic health.

Individual Variability and Personalized Approaches:

Recognize the individual variability in metabolic responses to the ketogenic diet. Explore the importance of personalized approaches, considering factors such as genetics, lifestyle, and health status. Understand how tailoring the ketogenic approach can optimize outcomes for insulin sensitivity and blood sugar regulation.

Metabolic Adaptation: Lipolysis and Fatty Acid Oxidation

In this section, we unravel the metabolic adaptation within the ketogenic journey, focusing on the dynamic processes of lipolysis and fatty acid oxidation that define the body's transition to a state of efficient fat utilization.

Lipolysis: Unlocking Fat Stores:

Embark on the intricate process of lipolysis—the unlocking of fat stores for energy. Explore how the ketogenic diet triggers the release of stored triglycerides, breaking them down into fatty acids and glycerol. Understand the role of hormones, particularly insulin and glucagon, in regulating this process and initiating the flow of fatty acids into the bloodstream.

Fatty Acid Oxidation: The Cellular Powerhouse:

Delve into the cellular powerhouse of fatty acid oxidation—a cornerstone of energy production in ketosis. Explore how fatty acids, liberated through lipolysis, enter the mitochondria to undergo beta-oxidation. Understand the stepwise breakdown of fatty acids into acetyl-CoA, fueling the production of ATP—the cellular currency of energy.

Ketogenesis: Synthesizing Ketone Bodies:

Uncover the synthesis of ketone bodies through ketogenesis—a key outcome of enhanced fatty acid oxidation. Explore how acetyl-CoA produced from fatty acids gives rise to ketones, including beta-hydroxybutyrate, acetoacetate, and acetone. Understand the liver's role in ketone synthesis and the subsequent release of ketones into the bloodstream for energy utilization.

Enhanced Fat Utilization in Ketosis:

Navigate the enhanced fat utilization that characterizes ketosis. Explore how the metabolic adaptation to the ketogenic diet optimizes the body's ability to use fats as a primary source of energy. Understand the shift from glucose-centric metabolism to a state where fats, both dietary and stored, become the predominant fuel for various tissues, including muscles and the brain.

Regulation by Hormones: Insulin and Glucagon Dance:

Dive into the intricate dance between insulin and glucagon—hormones that regulate lipolysis and fatty acid oxidation. Explore how insulin inhibits lipolysis and promotes fat storage, while glucagon stimulates lipolysis and enhances fatty acid oxidation. Understand the delicate balance orchestrated by these hormones to maintain metabolic equilibrium.

Adaptation and Metabolic Flexibility:

Examine the concept of metabolic flexibility—an adaptive response that allows the body to seamlessly transition between fuel sources. Explore how the ketogenic lifestyle fosters metabolic flexibility, enabling efficient utilization of both carbohydrates and fats based on dietary intake and energy demands. Understand the implications for sustained energy production and resilience.

Nutritional Components of Ketogenic Diet: Crafting a Nourishing Paradigm

In this section, we delve into the nutritional components that form the foundation of the ketogenic diet. Explore the optimal ratios of macronutrients, delve into micronutrient considerations, and understand how this carefully crafted nutritional paradigm contributes to sustained ketosis and overall well-being.

Macronutrient Ratios: Striking the Balance

Embark on a journey into the world of macronutrient ratios within the ketogenic framework. Explore the optimal balance of fats, proteins, and carbohydrates that characterize a well-formulated ketogenic diet. Understand the science behind each macronutrient's role in supporting ketosis, metabolic health, and overall nutritional adequacy.

Micronutrient Considerations: Beyond Macros

Navigate through the micronutrient landscape, understanding the importance of vitamins, minerals, and other essential nutrients within the ketogenic lifestyle. Explore the role of micronutrients in supporting overall well-being, and metabolic processes, and addressing potential nutrient gaps that may arise from dietary restrictions.

Balancing Fats, Proteins, and Carbohydrates:

Delve into the nuanced art of balancing fats, proteins, and carbohydrates to maintain ketosis. Explore the optimal macronutrient ratios that align with individual goals, metabolic status, and activity levels. Understand the impact of varying these ratios on energy production, satiety, and the body's adaptation to sustained fat utilization.

Nutrient-Dense Fat Sources:

Explore nutrient-dense sources of fats within the ketogenic diet. From avocados and nuts to olive oil and fatty fish, understand the importance of incorporating a diverse range of healthy fats to ensure a spectrum of essential fatty acids, vitamins, and antioxidants. Discover how these fats contribute to both nutritional and metabolic well-being.

Sufficient Protein for Muscle Health:

Understand the role of protein in supporting muscle health within the ketogenic lifestyle. Explore the importance of choosing high-quality protein sources to provide essential amino acids and promote muscle maintenance. Gain insights into determining the right protein intake to align with individual needs and goals.

Fiber-rich Low-Carbohydrate Vegetables:

Navigate the realm of fiber-rich, low-carbohydrate vegetables that play a crucial role in providing essential nutrients and promoting digestive health within the ketogenic diet. Explore a variety of non-starchy vegetables that contribute fiber, vitamins, and minerals without jeopardizing ketosis.

Micronutrient-Rich Foods:

Delve into micronutrient-rich foods that complement the ketogenic lifestyle. From leafy greens and cruciferous vegetables to organ meats and dairy, explore diverse options that offer a spectrum of vitamins and minerals essential for overall health. Understand how strategic food choices contribute to nutritional adequacy.

Macronutrient Ratios: Crafting the Ketogenic Symphony

In this section, we explore the art and science of macronutrient ratios within the ketogenic framework. Understand the optimal balance of fats, proteins, and carbohydrates that characterizes a well-formulated ketogenic diet, ensuring a symphony of nutrients that supports ketosis, metabolic health, and overall well-being.

The Ketogenic Triad: Fats, Proteins, and Carbohydrates:

Embark on a journey through the ketogenic triad—fats, proteins, and carbohydrates—each playing a vital role in sculpting the macronutrient landscape. Explore the unique contributions of each component, understanding how they synergize to create an environment conducive to sustained ketosis.

Fat as the Primary Energy Source:

Delve into the principle of fat as the primary energy source within the ketogenic diet. Understand how the majority of daily caloric intake comes from healthy fats, including sources like avocados, nuts, seeds, and oils. Explore the metabolic benefits of relying on fats for sustained energy and ketone production.

Protein for Muscle Maintenance:

Navigate the role of protein in the context of muscle health within the ketogenic lifestyle. Explore the importance of sufficient protein intake to provide essential amino acids, support muscle maintenance, and contribute to overall body composition. Understand the balance between optimizing protein intake and maintaining ketosis.

Striking the Right Balance:

Explore the nuanced art of striking the right balance between fats, proteins, and carbohydrates to maintain ketosis. Understand the recommended macronutrient ratios, such as high fat, moderate protein, and low carbohydrate distribution. Gain insights into tailoring these ratios based on individual goals, metabolic status, and activity levels.

Customization Based on Individual Goals:

Recognize the importance of customization based on individual goals within the ketogenic framework. Whether pursuing weight loss, muscle gain, or specific health outcomes, understand how adjusting macronutrient ratios can align with diverse objectives. Explore practical strategies for tailoring the ketogenic diet to meet personal aspirations.

Monitoring and Adjusting Macronutrient Intake:

Delve into the importance of monitoring and adjusting macronutrient intake to optimize ketosis and overall well-being. Explore methods for tracking macronutrients, including apps and food diaries. Understand the flexibility of adjusting ratios based on feedback from individual responses, ensuring a personalized and effective approach.

Addressing Potential Challenges:

Navigate potential challenges associated with macronutrient ratios within the ketogenic diet. Explore common issues such as overemphasis on fats, inadequate protein intake, or difficulty in reaching ketosis. Gain insights into troubleshooting strategies, ensuring a balanced and sustainable approach to macronutrient consumption.

Micronutrient Considerations: Nurturing Vitality Beyond Macros

In this section, we delve into the realm of micronutrient considerations within the ketogenic lifestyle. Explore the importance of vitamins, minerals, and essential nutrients, ensuring a holistic approach to nutrition that supports overall well-being.

Essential Micronutrients for Vibrant Health:

Embark on a journey through the essential micronutrients that play a pivotal role in supporting vibrant health within the ketogenic diet. Explore the significance of vitamins, minerals, and other vital nutrients, understanding their diverse functions in metabolic processes, immune function, and overall physiological well-being.

Balancing Micronutrient Intake:

Navigate the art of balancing micronutrient intake to address potential gaps that may arise from dietary restrictions within the ketogenic lifestyle. Explore a variety of nutrient-dense foods, including vegetables, nuts, seeds, and organ meats, to ensure a broad spectrum of essential micronutrients. Understand the role of diversity in food choices for optimal nutrient absorption.

Vitamins and Minerals in Ketogenic Foods:

Delve into the rich array of vitamins and minerals present in ketogenic foods. From leafy greens and cruciferous vegetables to nuts, seeds, and fatty fish, explore diverse sources that contribute to micronutrient abundance. Gain insights into the specific vitamins and minerals critical for various physiological functions.

Electrolytes and Fluid Balance:

Explore the importance of electrolytes in maintaining fluid balance within the ketogenic lifestyle. Understand the role of sodium, potassium, magnesium, and calcium in supporting hydration, muscle function, and nerve signaling. Gain insights into strategies for ensuring adequate electrolyte intake, especially during the initial stages of ketosis.

Considerations for Bone Health:

Navigate considerations for bone health within the context of the ketogenic diet. Explore the role of calcium and vitamin D in maintaining strong and healthy bones. Understand how strategic food choices and, if necessary, supplementation can contribute to optimal bone mineralization.

Individual Variability and Micronutrient Needs:

Recognize individual variability in micronutrient needs and absorption. Explore factors such as age, gender, health status, and genetic variations that influence how the body processes and utilizes micronutrients. Understand the importance of personalized approaches to meet individual requirements.

Supplementation Strategies:

Delve into supplementation strategies when addressing specific micronutrient needs within the ketogenic lifestyle. Explore instances where supplementation may be beneficial, such as with vitamin D, B vitamins, or electrolytes. Understand the importance of consulting healthcare professionals for personalized guidance on supplementation.

Getting Started: Embarking on Your Ketogenic Journey

In this section, we guide you through the initial steps of embarking on your ketogenic journey. From understanding the basics to practical tips for implementation, prepare to transition into the transformative world of ketogenic living.

Understanding the Basics:

Embark on your ketogenic journey by understanding the basics of the lifestyle. Explore the principles of ketosis, the role of macronutrients, and the science behind the ketogenic diet. Gain insights into the metabolic changes that occur during ketosis and the potential benefits for overall health and well-being.

Setting Personal Goals:

Define your personal goals within the ketogenic framework. Whether aiming for weight loss, improved energy levels, or specific health outcomes, establish clear and achievable objectives. Understand how tailoring the ketogenic approach to your unique goals can enhance motivation and guide your journey.

Creating a Ketogenic Meal Plan:

Dive into the art of creating a ketogenic meal plan that aligns with your macronutrient goals and preferences. Explore a variety of nutrient-dense foods, including healthy fats, high-quality proteins, and low-carbohydrate vegetables. Gain practical tips for meal prepping and ensuring a diverse and enjoyable culinary experience.

Navigating Food Choices:

Navigate the world of ketogenic food choices, from whole foods to keto-friendly snacks. Explore a spectrum of nutrient-dense options that contribute to macronutrient balance and micronutrient richness. Understand how to make informed choices when dining out or facing different social situations.

Overcoming Challenges:

Address potential challenges that may arise during the initial stages of adopting a ketogenic lifestyle. Explore strategies for overcoming keto flu symptoms, managing cravings, and staying consistent with your dietary choices. Gain insights into troubleshooting common issues to ensure a smooth transition.

Incorporating Physical Activity:

Understand the role of physical activity within the ketogenic lifestyle. Explore how exercise can complement your goals, enhance metabolic flexibility, and contribute to overall well-being. Gain insights into adapting your workout routine to align with the unique energy demands of a ketogenic metabolism.

Monitoring Progress:

Learn how to effectively monitor your progress within the ketogenic journey. Explore methods for tracking macronutrients, measuring ketone levels, and assessing changes in energy, mood, and body composition. Understand the importance of both quantitative and qualitative feedback in gauging success.

Seeking Support and Resources:

Recognize the value of seeking support and accessing resources as you embark on your ketogenic journey. Explore online communities, books, and reputable websites that provide guidance, recipes, and success stories. Understand the importance of a supportive environment in fostering motivation and adherence.

Assessing Personal Health and Goals: Charting Your Ketogenic Path

In this subsection, we delve into the crucial process of assessing your health and goals within the ketogenic framework. By understanding your unique circumstances and aspirations, you can tailor the ketogenic approach to optimize your well-being.

Understanding Your Current Health Status:

Embark on the journey of assessing your current health status. Consider factors such as medical history, existing health conditions, and any medications you may be taking. Consult with healthcare professionals if needed to ensure that the ketogenic lifestyle aligns with your individual health needs and goals.

Defining Your Personal Goals:

Define your personal goals within the context of the ketogenic lifestyle. Whether your focus is on weight management, improved energy levels, or specific health outcomes, articulate clear and achievable objectives. Understanding your goals will guide the customization of your ketogenic approach to meet your unique aspirations.

Exploring Weight Management Objectives:

If weight management is a primary goal, delve into the specifics of your objectives. Consider desired weight loss or maintenance targets, and understand how the ketogenic approach can support effective and sustainable outcomes. Explore the nuances of adjusting macronutrient ratios to align with your weight management goals.

Assessing Energy and Fitness Goals:

If energy levels and fitness are central to your goals, assess your current physical activity levels and aspirations. Explore how the ketogenic lifestyle can enhance energy production, support endurance, and contribute to overall fitness. Understand the adaptability of your workout routine to align with the unique energy demands of ketosis.

Navigating Health Conditions:

Navigate any pre-existing health conditions you may have and assess how the ketogenic lifestyle might impact them. Consider conditions such as diabetes, metabolic disorders, or neurological issues. Consult with healthcare professionals to ensure a comprehensive understanding of how ketosis may influence your specific health circumstances.

Considering Hormonal and Women's Health Goals:

For women, consider hormonal and reproductive health goals within the ketogenic context. Explore how the diet may influence menstrual cycles, hormonal balance, and reproductive health. Understand the importance of customization to address women's unique physiological considerations within the ketogenic lifestyle.

Personalizing Your Ketogenic Approach:

Based on your health assessment and defined goals, personalize your ketogenic approach. Consider variations in macronutrient ratios, meal timing, and food choices that align with your individual needs. Embrace the flexibility inherent in the ketogenic lifestyle to optimize outcomes and ensure a sustainable and enjoyable journey.

Health Checkup and Consultation: Foundations of Personalized Well-being

Embark on the foundational step of a health checkup and consultation as you chart your path within the ketogenic lifestyle. This section emphasizes the importance of understanding your current health status and seeking professional guidance to ensure a personalized and safe approach.

Prioritizing Your Well-being:

Make your well-being a priority by initiating a comprehensive health checkup. Schedule an appointment with healthcare professionals to assess your current health status, including factors such as medical history, existing conditions, and medications. Prioritize open communication to ensure a collaborative approach to your health journey.

Consulting Healthcare Professionals:

Engage in meaningful consultations with healthcare professionals, including physicians, registered dietitians, or nutritionists. Seek guidance on the compatibility of the ketogenic lifestyle with your health circumstances. Share your goals, concerns, and any specific health conditions to receive personalized advice tailored to your unique needs.

Blood Tests and Biomarker Analysis:

Consider the value of blood tests and biomarker analysis as part of your health checkup. Assess key indicators such as lipid profiles, blood glucose levels, and inflammation markers. Understanding these biomarkers provides insights into metabolic health and informs adjustments to your ketogenic approach for optimal well-being.

Discussing Medications and Supplements:

During your consultation, discuss any medications you are currently taking and inquire about potential interactions with the ketogenic lifestyle. Seek guidance on adjusting medication dosages if needed. Explore the role of supplements to address specific nutrient needs and ensure a balanced nutritional profile within the ketogenic framework.

Addressing Health Concerns and Risks:

Openly discuss any health concerns or potential risks associated with the ketogenic lifestyle. Address considerations such as cardiovascular health, liver function, and electrolyte balance. Healthcare professionals can provide valuable insights into mitigating risks and optimizing the ketogenic approach to align with your health goals.

Establishing Long-Term Health Monitoring:

Work with healthcare professionals to establish a plan for long-term health monitoring. Schedule regular checkups and follow-up appointments to track your progress, assess any changes in health markers, and make informed adjustments to your ketogenic approach. Create a collaborative partnership for sustained well-being.

Gaining Clarity on Ketogenic Adaptation:

Seek clarity on the process of ketogenic adaptation and potential physiological changes. Understand how the body transitions into ketosis, the expected timeline for adaptation, and common experiences during this phase. Healthcare professionals can provide guidance on managing potential challenges and optimizing adaptation.

Defining Individual Goals and Objectives: Crafting Your Ketogenic Path

In this subsection, we focus on the crucial step of defining individual goals and objectives within the ketogenic framework. By articulating clear and achievable goals, you lay the foundation for a personalized and purposeful journey toward well-being.

Clarifying Weight Management Objectives:

Begin by clarifying your weight management objectives within the ketogenic context. Define whether your goal is weight loss, maintenance, or specific body composition changes. Set realistic and achievable targets, considering factors such as your starting point, timeline, and desired outcomes.

Setting Measurable Targets:

Ensure that your goals are measurable, allowing you to track progress and celebrate milestones. Define specific metrics, such as pounds or kilograms lost, body fat percentage changes, or clothing size adjustments. Measurable targets provide clarity and motivation throughout your ketogenic journey.

Exploring Energy and Fitness Aspirations:

Explore your energy and fitness aspirations within the ketogenic lifestyle. Define how you envision your energy levels, endurance, and overall fitness improving. Consider specific fitness goals, whether related to cardiovascular health, strength training, or athletic performance. Align your ketogenic approach with these aspirations.

Aligning with Health and Wellness Goals:

Align your ketogenic journey with broader health and wellness goals. Consider aspects such as improved metabolic health, stabilized blood sugar levels, enhanced cognitive function, or hormonal balance. Define the specific health outcomes that resonate with your well-being objectives.

Addressing Hormonal and Women's Health Goals:

For women, address hormonal and reproductive health goals within the ketogenic framework. Consider how the diet may influence menstrual cycles, hormonal balance, and reproductive well-being. Define specific objectives related to women's health, ensuring a holistic approach to your ketogenic journey.

Customizing Goals Based on Individual Needs:

Recognize the importance of customizing goals based on individual needs and preferences. Tailor your ketogenic approach to align with your unique circumstances, including lifestyle, preferences, and any specific considerations. Ensure that your goals are meaningful and realistic within the context of your life.

Prioritizing Sustainable and Enjoyable Outcomes:

Prioritize goals that are sustainable and enjoyable in the long term. Consider how your ketogenic journey can integrate seamlessly into your lifestyle, promoting adherence and overall well-being. Define outcomes that bring not only physical benefits but also a sense of fulfillment and satisfaction.

Seeking Support and Accountability:

Consider seeking support and accountability in defining and pursuing your goals. Share your objectives with friends, family, or members of the ketogenic community who can provide encouragement and motivation. Establish accountability mechanisms to stay on track and celebrate achievements together.

Transitioning into Ketogenic Lifestyle: Navigating the Transformation

In this section, we guide you through the transformative process of transitioning into the ketogenic lifestyle. From understanding the basics to practical tips for a seamless shift, prepare to embark on a journey that aligns with your goals and fosters well-being.

Understanding the Basics of Ketogenic Lifestyle:

Begin your transition by solidifying your understanding of the basics of the ketogenic lifestyle. Revisit the principles of ketosis, the role of macronutrients, and the science behind the ketogenic diet. Enhance your knowledge of how the body adapts to ketosis and the potential benefits for overall health.

Assessing Current Dietary Habits:

Assess your current dietary habits as a crucial step in transitioning to keto. Reflect on your typical macronutrient intake, food choices, and meal patterns. Identify areas where adjustments can be made to align with the macronutrient ratios characteristic of the ketogenic diet.

Gradual Reduction of Carbohydrates:

Initiate the transition by gradually reducing your carbohydrate intake. This approach helps minimize potential discomfort associated with a sudden shift. Start by reducing high-carbohydrate foods, such as grains, sugars, and starchy vegetables, while increasing healthy fats and moderate protein.

Incorporating Healthy Fats:

Embrace the inclusion of healthy fats as a central component of your ketogenic transition. Explore a variety of sources, including avocados, nuts, seeds, olive oil, and fatty fish. Adjust your meals to prioritize fats as the primary energy source, supporting the metabolic shift toward ketosis.

Exploring Keto-Friendly Proteins:

Opt for keto-friendly protein sources to meet your protein needs while minimizing carbohydrate intake. Include options such as poultry, fish, eggs, and high-quality meats. Be mindful of protein intake to maintain the balance required for ketosis while supporting muscle health.

Navigating Low-Carbohydrate Vegetables:

Incorporate low-carbohydrate vegetables to provide essential nutrients and dietary fiber. Explore a diverse range of non-starchy vegetables, including leafy greens, cruciferous vegetables, and colorful options. These vegetables contribute to overall health while aligning with the low-carbohydrate nature of the ketogenic lifestyle.

Staying Hydrated and Addressing Electrolytes:

Prioritize hydration during the transition, ensuring an adequate intake of water throughout the day. Address electrolyte needs by incorporating sources of sodium, potassium, magnesium, and calcium. This is particularly important during the initial stages of ketosis to prevent electrolyte imbalances.

Monitoring and Adjusting Based on Feedback:

Regularly monitor your progress and adjust your approach based on feedback from your body. Pay attention to energy levels, mood, satiety, and any signs of ketosis, such as increased ketone levels. Fine-tune your macronutrient ratios and food choices to optimize your ketogenic experience.

Seeking Support and Sharing Goals:

Seek support from friends, family, or the ketogenic community as you transition. Share your goals and experiences to foster encouragement and accountability. Leverage online resources, forums, and social media groups to connect with others on a similar journey.

Gradual vs. Immediate Transition: Tailoring Your Shift to Ketogenic Living

In this subsection, we explore the considerations between a gradual and immediate transition into the ketogenic lifestyle. Understanding the nuances of each approach allows you to tailor your shift based on your preferences, goals, and individual circumstances.

Gradual Transition: A Gentle Shift:

Opting for a gradual transition involves slowly reducing carbohydrate intake over an extended period. This approach allows your body to adapt more comfortably to the changes associated with ketosis. Consider the following aspects:

- Reducing Carbohydrates Incrementally: Gradually decrease high-carbohydrate foods, giving your body time to adjust to lower carbohydrate levels.

- Phasing In Healthy Fats: Introduce healthy fats gradually, allowing your taste buds and digestive system to acclimate to the increased fat content in your meals.

- Monitoring Responses: Pay close attention to how your body responds to the changes. Adjust your carbohydrate, fat, and protein ratios based on feedback, optimizing the transition process.

Immediate Transition: Embracing the Change Rapidly:

Opting for an immediate transition involves a swift shift to a ketogenic lifestyle. This approach may be suitable for individuals who prefer decisiveness and are motivated by quick results. Consider the following aspects:

- Clearing Carbohydrate-Rich Foods: Remove high-carbohydrate foods from your diet promptly to initiate a rapid shift into ketosis.

- Emphasizing Healthy Fats Early: Prioritize healthy fats as a primary energy source right from the start. This helps signal the body to transition to utilizing fats for fuel.

- Mindful Electrolyte Management: Given the potential for a faster onset of ketosis, pay extra attention to electrolyte balance to mitigate symptoms like the keto flu.

Factors Influencing Your Decision:

Consider the following factors when deciding between a gradual or immediate transition:

- Personal Preferences: Reflect on your preferences and tolerance for change. Some individuals may prefer a gentle introduction, while others thrive on quick shifts.

- Motivation Levels: Assess your motivation and readiness to embrace a ketogenic lifestyle. Immediate transition may be motivating for some, while others may find gradual changes more sustainable.

- Health Considerations: Take into account any existing health conditions, dietary restrictions, or medical advice. Consult with healthcare professionals to determine the most suitable transition approach for your health circumstances.

Customizing Your Approach:

Recognize that the effectiveness of either approach depends on individual factors. You can also customize your transition by incorporating elements of both gradual and immediate strategies based on your unique needs and preferences.

Overcoming Initial Challenges: Strategies for Success in the Early Stages

In this section, we provide strategies to overcome common challenges encountered during the initial stages of transitioning into the ketogenic lifestyle. By addressing these challenges proactively, you can enhance your experience and increase the likelihood of long-term success.

Navigating the Keto Flu:

Understanding Keto Flu: The keto flu refers to a collection of symptoms, including fatigue, headache, nausea, and irritability, that some individuals may experience during the early stages of ketosis.

Strategies for Relief:

- Hydration: Ensure proper hydration to counteract potential dehydration associated with the diuretic effect of ketosis.

- Electrolyte Supplementation: Increase your intake of sodium, potassium, and magnesium to address electrolyte imbalances.

- Gradual Transition: Consider a gradual transition to minimize the intensity of symptoms.

Managing Cravings and Hunger:

Understanding Cravings: Cravings for familiar carbohydrate-rich foods are common during the initial stages of the ketogenic lifestyle.

Strategies for Success:

- Satiating Fats: Prioritize foods rich in healthy fats to enhance satiety and reduce cravings.

- Protein Intake: Include an adequate amount of protein in your meals to support feelings of fullness.

- Mindful Eating: Practice mindful eating to distinguish between true hunger and emotional cravings.

Adapting to Changes in Digestion:

Understanding Digestive Changes: Some individuals may experience changes in bowel habits, including constipation or diarrhea, as the body adjusts to the ketogenic diet.

Strategies for Comfort:

- Hydration and Fiber: Ensure sufficient hydration and incorporate fiber-rich low-carbohydrate vegetables to support digestive health.

- Probiotics: Consider incorporating probiotic-rich foods or supplements to promote a healthy gut microbiome.

- Balanced Fats: Ensure a balance of saturated and unsaturated fats to support digestive processes.

Addressing Social and Practical Considerations:

Understanding Social Challenges: Social situations and practical considerations can pose challenges, especially when dining out or attending events.

Strategies for Success:

- Communication: Communicate your dietary preferences and restrictions to friends and family to garner support.

- Menu Planning: Plan meals ahead of time and, when dining out, choose keto-friendly options from menus.

- Flexibility: Be adaptable and find creative solutions to navigate social gatherings while staying true to your goals.

Monitoring and Adjusting:

Understanding Individual Responses: Individuals may respond differently to the ketogenic lifestyle, requiring ongoing monitoring and adjustments.

Strategies for Optimization:

- Regular Check-ins: Regularly assess your energy levels, mood, and overall well-being.

- Tracking Macros: Use tools to track macronutrient intake and adjust ratios based on your responses.

- Professional Guidance: Consult with healthcare professionals or nutrition experts for personalized advice.

Setting Realistic Expectations: A Foundation for Success

In this section, we emphasize the importance of setting realistic expectations as you embark on your ketogenic journey. By establishing achievable goals and understanding the dynamics of the process, you pave the way for a successful and sustainable experience.

Understanding the Nature of Change:

Recognize that transitioning into the ketogenic lifestyle involves a significant dietary shift and metabolic adaptation. Understand that changes in energy levels, satiety, and body composition may take time. Acknowledge that individual responses vary, and progress is often gradual.

Establishing Short-Term Goals:

Set short-term, achievable goals that align with your broader objectives. Focus on milestones such as adhering to daily macronutrient targets, successfully navigating social situations, or managing cravings effectively. Celebrate these smaller victories to stay motivated on your journey.

Embracing the Learning Curve:

Acknowledge that adopting a new way of eating involves a learning curve. Familiarize yourself with keto-friendly foods, experiment with recipes, and discover what works best for your preferences and lifestyle. Embrace the opportunity to expand your culinary skills and nutritional knowledge.

Recognizing Individual Variability:

Understand that individual responses to the ketogenic lifestyle vary. Factors such as metabolism, genetics, and pre-existing health conditions can influence outcomes. Be open to adjusting your approach based on personal feedback and consult with healthcare professionals for tailored guidance.

Considering Non-Scale Achievements:

Broaden your definition of success beyond the scale. Recognize non-scale achievements, such as improved energy levels, enhanced mental clarity, or positive changes in overall well-being. Emphasize the holistic benefits of the ketogenic lifestyle beyond numerical metrics.

Patience in Adaptation and Results:

Exercise patience as your body adapts to the ketogenic lifestyle. Understand that metabolic changes, including ketosis and fat adaptation, may take time. Avoid comparing your progress to others and focus on your journey. Consistency and persistence are key to long-term success.

Adjusting Expectations for Challenges:

Anticipate and adjust expectations for potential challenges. Recognize that you may encounter obstacles such as the keto flu, cravings, or social situations. Approach challenges as opportunities to learn, adapt, and refine your strategies for long-term success.

Seeking Support and Accountability:

Engage in a supportive network or seek accountability partners to share your journey. Having individuals who understand your goals and provide encouragement can be invaluable. Share both successes and challenges, fostering a sense of community and motivation.

Celebrating Progress Along the Way:

Celebrate milestones and progress throughout your ketogenic journey. Whether it's reaching a specific weight goal, mastering a new keto-friendly recipe, or consistently adhering to your dietary plan, take time to acknowledge and celebrate your achievements.

Short-Term vs. Long-Term Goals: Balancing Perspectives in Your Ketogenic Journey

In this subsection, we explore the dynamic interplay between short-term and long-term goals within the context of your ketogenic journey. Understanding how to balance and align these goals is crucial for sustained success and overall well-being.

Short-Term Goals: Immediate Wins and Milestones:

Embracing Adaptation: Set short-term goals that focus on the immediate adjustments and adaptations required during the initial stages of transitioning to a ketogenic lifestyle. These goals may include gradually reducing carbohydrate intake, increasing healthy fats, and navigating social situations while staying true to your dietary preferences.

Monitoring Energy and Well-Being: Prioritize short-term goals that involve monitoring your energy levels, mood, and overall well-being. Track your responses to dietary changes, identify patterns, and make necessary adjustments. Short-term wins may involve successfully managing cravings, maintaining ketosis, or mastering keto-friendly recipes.

Building Consistency: Use short-term goals to establish and reinforce consistency in your daily routines. This could involve adhering to specific macronutrient targets, practicing mindful eating, and incorporating regular physical activity. Short-term consistency lays the groundwork for long-term habits.

Long-Term Goals: Sustainable Well-Being and Transformations:

Achieving Desired Outcomes: Define long-term goals that align with your overarching aspirations for sustained well-being and transformative outcomes. These may include achieving and maintaining a target weight, optimizing metabolic health, and cultivating a lifestyle that supports overall wellness.

Cultivating Habits: Use long-term goals as a framework for cultivating habits that contribute to lasting success. Focus on building habits related to food choices, meal planning, and self-care practices. Sustainable habits contribute to the maintenance of ketosis and a positive relationship with your ketogenic lifestyle.

Enhancing Overall Quality of Life: Consider long-term goals that go beyond the physical aspects and encompass the enhancement of your overall quality of life. This could involve improvements in mental clarity, increased energy levels, and a sense of well-being. Strive for holistic well-being that extends beyond weight-related outcomes.

Balancing Perspectives:

Integration of Short-Term Wins: Acknowledge the role of short-term wins as integral components of your overall journey. Celebrate achievements and use them as building blocks for sustained progress. Short-term wins provide motivation, reinforce positive behaviors, and contribute to the momentum of your ketogenic experience.

Alignment with Long-Term Vision: Ensure that short-term goals align with and contribute to your long-term vision for well-being. Avoid approaches that sacrifice long-term sustainability for quick results. Seek a balance that fosters both immediate wins and a trajectory toward transformative, enduring outcomes.

Flexibility and Adaptability: Embrace flexibility and adaptability in your goal-setting approach. Recognize that your goals may evolve as you progress in your ketogenic journey. Be open to adjusting both short-term and long-term goals based on feedback, changing circumstances, and personal growth.

Monitoring Progress and Adjusting Expectations: A Dynamic Approach to Ketogenic Living

In this section, we explore the importance of monitoring your progress and being adaptable in your expectations as you navigate the complexities of the ketogenic lifestyle. By embracing a dynamic approach, you can optimize your experience and make informed adjustments along the way.

Establishing Monitoring Practices:

Tracking Macronutrients: Utilize tools and apps to track your daily macronutrient intake. Monitor your ratios of fats, proteins, and carbohydrates to ensure alignment with your ketogenic goals. Adjust these ratios based on your responses, energy levels, and metabolic needs.

Measuring Ketone Levels: Incorporate methods for measuring ketone levels, such as blood ketone meters or urine test strips. Regular ketone monitoring provides insights into your state of ketosis and allows you to make adjustments to your dietary approach accordingly.

Assessing Energy and Well-Being: Monitor your energy levels, mood, and overall well-being regularly. Pay attention to how your body responds to the ketogenic lifestyle, both in the short term and over extended periods. Assess changes in cognitive function, physical performance, and emotional resilience.

Adaptability and Adjustments:

Recognizing Individual Variability: Acknowledge that individual responses to the ketogenic lifestyle can vary. Be open to adjusting your approach based on your unique physiological responses, preferences, and health considerations. What works well for one person may require customization for another.

Fine-Tuning Macronutrient Ratios: Be willing to fine-tune your macronutrient ratios based on your goals and experiences. Adjust the proportions of fats, proteins, and carbohydrates to optimize your energy levels, satiety, and overall well-being. Experiment with different ratios to find what works best for you.

Addressing Challenges Proactively: Anticipate potential challenges and address them proactively. Whether it's overcoming stalls in weight loss, managing cravings, or navigating social situations, develop strategies to mitigate challenges. Seek support and guidance when needed to overcome obstacles effectively.

Regular Reflection and Goal Reassessment:

Scheduled Reflection: Schedule regular reflection periods to assess your progress, challenges, and successes. Use these moments to celebrate achievements, identify areas for improvement, and adjust your expectations based on your evolving insights and experiences.

Goal Reassessment: Periodically reassess your short-term and long-term goals. Consider whether your objectives remain relevant and achievable, and adjust them as needed. Embrace the flexibility to refine your goals based on changing circumstances and evolving aspirations.

Professional Guidance: Consult with healthcare professionals or nutrition experts for personalized guidance. Seek their input on adjusting expectations, optimizing your dietary approach, and addressing any health considerations that may impact your ketogenic journey.

Celebrating Non-Scale Achievements:

Broadening Success Metrics: Broaden your definition of success beyond numerical metrics. Celebrate non-scale achievements, such as improvements in energy levels, enhanced mental clarity, or positive changes in overall well-being. Recognize the holistic benefits of the ketogenic lifestyle.

Cultivating a Positive Mindset: Foster a positive mindset that appreciates the journey rather than focusing solely on outcomes. Embrace the learning process, and view challenges as opportunities for growth and adaptation. A resilient mindset contributes to long-term success.

Customizing Ketogenic Diet for Women: Personalizing Your Approach

In this section, we delve into the nuances of customizing the ketogenic diet specifically for women. By understanding the unique physiological considerations, hormonal influences, and individual preferences, you can tailor your ketogenic approach to optimize overall health and well-being.

Addressing Women's Hormonal Considerations:

Menstrual Cycle Awareness: Consider the impact of the ketogenic diet on the menstrual cycle. Some women may experience changes in menstrual regularity or hormonal balance. Monitor your menstrual cycle, and consult with healthcare professionals if you have concerns about its impact on reproductive health.

Balancing Hormones: Customize your ketogenic approach to support hormonal balance. Incorporate nutrient-dense foods that provide essential vitamins and minerals crucial for hormonal health. Emphasize a variety of vegetables, healthy fats, and proteins to ensure a well-rounded nutritional profile.

Potential Benefits for Women: Explore the potential benefits of the ketogenic diet for women, including improved insulin sensitivity, stabilized blood sugar levels, and enhanced energy. Understand how these benefits may positively influence hormonal balance and overall well-being.

Tailoring Macronutrient Ratios:

Flexible Macronutrient Ratios: Recognize the flexibility in macronutrient ratios within the ketogenic framework. While the standard ketogenic diet typically involves high fats, moderate protein, and low carbohydrates, consider adjusting these ratios based on individual goals, preferences, and hormonal considerations.

Protein Intake for Women: Women may benefit from slightly higher protein intake to support muscle health, especially for those engaged in regular physical activity. Customize your protein intake based on your activity levels, muscle mass goals, and individual preferences.

Adapting Carbohydrate Levels: Explore variations in carbohydrate intake based on your response to ketosis. Some women may find that a slightly higher carbohydrate intake, within the ketogenic range, aligns better with their energy needs and hormonal balance. Experiment with different levels to find what works best for you.

Nutrient-Dense Foods for Women:

Incorporating Nutrient-Rich Foods: Prioritize nutrient-dense foods to ensure optimal micronutrient intake. Include a variety of colorful vegetables, leafy greens, and berries to provide essential vitamins, minerals, and antioxidants. Customize your food choices to support overall health and address specific nutritional needs.

Healthy Fats for Hormonal Support: Emphasize healthy fats that support hormonal function. Include sources such as avocados, nuts, seeds, olive oil, and fatty fish. These fats contribute to the production of hormones and provide sustained energy, supporting women's unique physiological requirements.

Consideration of Omega-3 Fatty Acids: Pay attention to omega-3 fatty acids, which play a crucial role in hormonal balance and overall health. Incorporate fatty fish, flaxseeds, and chia seeds to ensure an adequate intake of these essential fatty acids.

Individualized Approaches:

Consultation with Healthcare Professionals: Consult with healthcare professionals, such as nutritionists or dietitians, for personalized guidance. Address any health concerns, dietary restrictions, or individual factors that may influence your ketogenic approach. A tailored plan can enhance the effectiveness and safety of the ketogenic lifestyle.

Monitoring and Adjusting Based on Feedback: Regularly monitor your responses to the ketogenic diet. Pay attention to energy levels, mood, hormonal changes, and overall well-being. Adjust your approach based on feedback to ensure a customized and sustainable ketogenic experience.

Listening to Your Body: Practice intuitive eating and listen to your body's signals. Be attuned to hunger and satiety cues, and make adjustments to your dietary choices accordingly. Customizing your ketogenic approach involves finding a balance that aligns with your body's needs and signals.

Women's Unique Nutritional Needs: Navigating the Path to Optimal Well-being

In this section, we explore the unique nutritional needs of women within the context of the ketogenic lifestyle. Understanding and addressing these needs is essential for optimizing overall health, hormonal balance, and well-being.

Key Considerations for Women's Nutrition:

Caloric Requirements: Recognize that women may have distinct caloric requirements based on factors such as age, activity level, and metabolic rate. Customizing your caloric intake within the ketogenic framework ensures that energy needs are met while aligning with individual goals.

Micronutrient Intake: Emphasize the importance of micronutrient intake to address women's specific nutritional needs. Include a variety of nutrient-dense foods such as vegetables, leafy greens, and berries to provide essential vitamins, minerals, and antioxidants crucial for overall health.

Iron and Folate: Pay attention to iron and folate intake, as these nutrients are particularly important for women's health. Incorporate sources such as lean meats, legumes, leafy greens, and fortified foods to support iron levels and folate requirements, especially during reproductive years.

Hormonal Health and Nutrient Support:

Omega-3 Fatty Acids: Prioritize omega-3 fatty acids to support hormonal health. Include fatty fish, flaxseeds, chia seeds, and walnuts in your ketogenic diet to ensure an adequate intake of these essential fatty acids, which play a crucial role in hormonal balance.

Calcium and Vitamin D: Address calcium and vitamin D needs for bone health, especially important for women. Include dairy or dairy alternatives, leafy greens, and fatty fish to support calcium intake. Exposure to sunlight is also crucial for natural vitamin D synthesis.

Protein for Muscle Health: Recognize the significance of protein for muscle health, particularly relevant for women engaged in regular physical activity. Customize your protein intake based on activity levels and individual goals to support muscle maintenance and growth.

Menstrual Cycle and Adaptations:

Nutritional Adaptations during Menstrual Phases: Acknowledge potential nutritional adaptations based on menstrual phases. Some women may experience changes in appetite, energy levels, and nutrient requirements during different phases of the menstrual cycle. Adjust your dietary choices to accommodate these variations.

Electrolyte Balance: Support electrolyte balance, especially during the menstrual cycle. Adequate intake of sodium, potassium, magnesium, and calcium becomes crucial to mitigate potential imbalances associated with hormonal fluctuations. Consider adjusting electrolyte-rich foods during these phases.

Pregnancy and Lactation:

Customizing for Pregnancy: If pregnant or planning for pregnancy, customize your ketogenic approach to ensure sufficient nutrient intake for both you and the developing fetus. Consult with healthcare professionals to establish a nutrition plan that meets the unique requirements of pregnancy.

Lactation and Nutrient Needs: For women in lactation, recognize the increased nutrient demands during breastfeeding. Ensure adequate intake of nutrients such as omega-3 fatty acids, calcium, iron, and protein to support both maternal and infant health.

Professional Guidance and Monitoring:

Consultation with Healthcare Professionals: Seek professional guidance from healthcare professionals, including obstetricians, nutritionists, or dietitians. Tailor your ketogenic approach based on individual health considerations, and receive personalized advice to navigate specific life stages.

Regular Monitoring and Adjustments: Regularly monitor your nutritional status and make adjustments based on individual responses and life stages. As women's health needs evolve, a dynamic approach to nutritional choices ensures ongoing support for optimal well-being.

Menstrual Cycle and Hormonal Fluctuations: Navigating Women's Health Dynamics

In this section, we delve into the impact of the menstrual cycle and hormonal fluctuations on women's health within the context of the ketogenic lifestyle. Understanding these dynamics allows for a tailored approach that aligns with the different phases of the menstrual cycle.

Menstrual Cycle Phases and Nutritional Considerations:

Menstrual Phase:

During the menstrual phase, women may experience changes in energy levels, mood, and nutrient requirements. Consider the following nutritional considerations:

- Iron-rich foods: Address potential iron loss during menstruation by incorporating iron-rich foods such as lean meats, legumes, and leafy greens. Adequate iron intake supports energy levels and prevents iron deficiency.

- Hydration: Prioritize hydration to compensate for fluid loss during menstruation. Ensure an adequate intake of water and electrolytes to support overall well-being.

Follicular Phase:

As the follicular phase begins, energy levels may increase. Nutritional considerations during this phase include:

- Balanced Nutrient Intake: Focus on a balanced intake of macronutrients, including healthy fats, proteins, and carbohydrates. Tailor your macronutrient ratios based on individual preferences and goals.

● Physical Activity: Leverage increased energy levels to engage in physical activity that aligns with your fitness goals. Customize exercise routines based on personal preferences and energy levels.

Ovulatory Phase:

The ovulatory phase is characterized by increased energy and a potential shift in nutrient preferences. Consider the following nutritional strategies:

● Protein Emphasis: Emphasize protein intake to support muscle health and recovery. Include sources such as lean meats, poultry, fish, and plant-based protein options.

● Healthy Fats: Prioritize healthy fats to provide sustained energy. Include sources such as avocados, nuts, seeds, and olive oil to support overall well-being.

Luteal Phase:

During the luteal phase, some women may experience changes in appetite, cravings, and mood. Nutritional considerations include:

● Balanced Carbohydrates: Customize carbohydrate intake based on individual responses. Some women may benefit from a slightly higher carbohydrate intake to address cravings and support mood.

● Serotonin-Supportive Foods: Include foods rich in tryptophan to support serotonin production. Options such as turkey, chicken, dairy, and seeds contribute to mood regulation.

Adapting to Individual Responses:

Mindful Observation: Practice mindful observation of your body's responses throughout the menstrual cycle. Pay attention to energy levels, cravings, and mood changes to inform nutritional choices.

Adaptation of Macronutrient Ratios: Be open to adapting macronutrient ratios based on individual preferences and responses during different menstrual phases. Customizing your approach allows for a more tailored and supportive ketogenic experience.

Hydration and Electrolyte Balance:

Hydration Strategies: Prioritize hydration throughout the menstrual cycle. Adequate water intake is essential for overall well-being and can help alleviate symptoms associated with hormonal fluctuations.

Electrolyte Management: Address potential electrolyte imbalances by incorporating foods rich in sodium, potassium, magnesium, and calcium. Electrolyte-rich choices support hydration and help mitigate symptoms such as bloating and fatigue.

Consultation with Healthcare Professionals:

Individualized Guidance: Consult with healthcare professionals, such as nutritionists or healthcare providers, for personalized guidance. Tailor your ketogenic approach based on individual health considerations, hormonal fluctuations, and specific needs.

Professional Support for Hormonal Health: Seek professional support to address hormonal health and menstrual cycle concerns. Healthcare providers can offer insights into managing symptoms and optimizing overall well-being.

Pregnancy and Ketogenic Diet: Nurturing Maternal and Fetal Well-being

In this section, we explore the considerations and adaptations required for women who are pregnant and considering or following a ketogenic diet. Understanding how to nurture maternal and fetal well-being is crucial during this significant life stage.

Key Considerations for Pregnant Women:

Consultation with Healthcare Professionals:

- Essential First Step: Prioritize consultation with healthcare professionals, including obstetricians and registered dietitians, before adopting or continuing a ketogenic diet during pregnancy.

- Individualized Guidance: Seek personalized guidance based on your unique health history, nutritional needs, and any specific considerations related to your pregnancy.

Balancing Nutrient Intake:

- Nutrient-Dense Foods: Emphasize nutrient-dense foods to ensure a well-rounded and comprehensive intake of essential vitamins and minerals.

- Folate and Iron: Pay specific attention to folate and iron intake, crucial for fetal development. Include sources such as leafy greens, legumes, lean meats, and fortified foods.

Adequate Caloric Intake:

- Caloric Requirements: Recognize the increased caloric needs during pregnancy. Ensure that your ketogenic approach supports adequate caloric intake to meet both maternal and fetal energy requirements.

Hydration and Electrolytes:

- Hydration: Prioritize hydration as it is essential for overall well-being and can help alleviate symptoms like constipation.

- Electrolyte Balance: Maintain electrolyte balance by incorporating foods rich in sodium, potassium, magnesium, and calcium.

Adapting Ketogenic Diet for Pregnancy:

Carbohydrate Intake:

- Flexible Approach: Adopt a flexible approach to carbohydrate intake. While the standard ketogenic diet is low in carbohydrates, consider adjusting the ratio to accommodate the increased energy needs during pregnancy.

- Whole Food Carbohydrates: Include whole food sources of carbohydrates such as vegetables, fruits, and legumes to provide additional fiber, vitamins, and minerals.

Protein and Healthy Fats:

- Adequate Protein: Ensure adequate protein intake to support maternal tissue maintenance and fetal growth. Include sources such as poultry, fish, lean meats, eggs, and plant-based protein options.

- Healthy Fats: Prioritize healthy fats for energy and hormonal support. Include sources like avocados, nuts, seeds, and olive oil.

Individualized Macronutrient Ratios:

- Tailored Approach: Customize your macronutrient ratios based on individual responses, preferences, and healthcare professional recommendations. Individualization allows for a more adaptive and supportive ketogenic experience during pregnancy.

Monitoring and Adjustments:

Regular Monitoring:

- Maternal Well-being: Regularly monitor your own well-being, energy levels, and overall health. Pay attention to any signs of nutrient deficiencies or imbalances.

- Professional Monitoring: Undergo regular monitoring by healthcare professionals to assess fetal growth, maternal health, and overall progress. Professional guidance is crucial for ensuring the well-being of both mother and baby.

Adaptations Based on Feedback:

- Adapt to Changes: Be open to adapting your ketogenic approach based on feedback from healthcare professionals and your own experiences. Adjustments may be necessary to address changing nutritional needs and ensure optimal outcomes.

Mindful Eating and Enjoyable Choices:

- Mindful Food Choices: Practice mindful eating and make enjoyable food choices that align with both your ketogenic goals and nutritional needs during pregnancy.

- Celebrating Variety: Celebrate a variety of foods to ensure a broad spectrum of nutrients. Enjoying a diverse range of whole foods contributes to overall nutritional well-being.

Adjusting Macronutrient Ratios: Fine-Tuning Your Ketogenic Approach

In this section, we delve into the nuances of adjusting macronutrient ratios within the ketogenic framework. Fine-tuning your approach based on individual goals, preferences, and responses is essential for optimizing the benefits of the ketogenic lifestyle.

Understanding Macronutrient Ratios:

Standard Ketogenic Ratios:

- High Fat, Moderate Protein, Low Carbohydrates: The standard ketogenic approach typically involves high fat, moderate protein, and low carbohydrate intake. This ratio promotes ketosis, where the body utilizes fats for energy.

Customization Principles:

Individual Goals:

- Weight Loss vs. Maintenance: Adjust macronutrient ratios based on your specific goals. A higher fat ratio may be suitable for those aiming for weight loss, while a more moderate fat intake may be chosen for weight maintenance.

Activity Levels:

- Protein for Muscle Health: Consider your activity levels and fitness goals. Those engaging in regular physical activity may benefit from slightly higher protein intake to support muscle health and recovery.

Metabolic Variability:

- Metabolism and Adaptation: Recognize metabolic variability among individuals. Some may thrive with higher fat ratios, while others may find success with slightly higher protein or moderate carbohydrate intake. Experimentation can help determine what works best for you.

Adapting for Health Conditions:

Metabolic Conditions:

- Insulin Sensitivity: Individuals with insulin sensitivity concerns may benefit from a lower carbohydrate intake to support blood sugar control. Adjusting macronutrient ratios can be a valuable strategy in managing metabolic conditions.

Medical Consultation:

- Professional Guidance: Consult with healthcare professionals, especially in the presence of medical conditions. A healthcare provider or nutritionist can provide personalized advice based on your health status and goals.

Fine-Tuning for Hormonal Balance:

Women's Health Considerations:

- Hormonal Impact: Consider hormonal influences, especially for women. Some may find adjustments to macronutrient ratios beneficial during different phases of the menstrual cycle to support energy levels and well-being.

Omega-3 Fatty Acids:

- Hormonal Support: Prioritize omega-3 fatty acids for hormonal support. Include sources such as fatty fish, flaxseeds, and chia seeds to enhance the balance of essential fatty acids.

Adjusting Based on Feedback:

Energy Levels and Satiation:

- Balancing Fats for Satiety: Assess how different fat ratios impact your sense of satiety. Balancing fats, including both saturated and unsaturated fats, can contribute to sustained energy levels and satisfaction.

Experimentation and Observation:

- Personalized Approach: Experiment with variations in macronutrient ratios and observe how your body responds. Pay attention to energy levels, mood, and overall well-being to refine your personalized ketogenic approach.

Long-Term Sustainability:

Flexibility and Enjoyment:

- Balancing Enjoyment: Find a balance that allows for the enjoyment of food while still aligning with your ketogenic goals. A sustainable approach is one that you can maintain in the long term.

Cyclical Ketogenic Approaches:

- Carb Cycling: Explore cyclical ketogenic approaches, such as carb cycling, where carbohydrate intake varies on specific days. This can be beneficial for athletes or those seeking metabolic flexibility.

Professional Guidance:

Consultation with Experts:

- Nutritional Guidance: Seek guidance from nutritionists, dietitians, or healthcare professionals. Their expertise can provide insights into adjusting macronutrient ratios based on your individual needs and health considerations.

Regular Monitoring:

- Assessing Responses: Regularly monitor your responses to macronutrient adjustments. Track changes in weight, body composition, energy levels, and overall well-being to make informed decisions.

Protein Intake for Muscle Health: Optimizing Your Ketogenic Approach

In this subsection, we delve into the importance of protein intake for muscle health within the ketogenic framework. Understanding how to optimize protein consumption contributes to muscle maintenance, recovery, and overall well-being.

Role of Protein in Ketogenic Living:

Muscle Maintenance and Repair:

- Essential Building Blocks: Protein serves as the essential building block for muscle maintenance and repair. Adequate protein intake is crucial for supporting lean muscle mass, especially for individuals engaging in regular physical activity.

Energy Source and Metabolism:

- Glucose Production: In the absence of sufficient carbohydrates, the body can convert amino acids from protein into glucose through a process called gluconeogenesis. This provides an alternative energy source for various bodily functions.

Customizing Protein Intake:

Individualized Needs:

- Activity Levels and Goals: Customize your protein intake based on your activity levels, fitness goals, and overall health. Those involved in intense physical activity or seeking muscle growth may require higher protein intake compared to sedentary individuals.

Lean Body Mass Consideration:

- Lean Body Mass vs. Total Body Weight: Tailor protein intake to your lean body mass rather than total body weight. This approach accounts for variations in body composition and ensures a more accurate reflection of protein needs for muscle health.

Women's Protein Considerations:

Muscle Health for Women:

- Hormonal Impact: Consider hormonal influences on muscle health, especially for women. Adequate protein intake supports hormonal balance and contributes to overall well-being.

Active Women and Protein Needs:

- Regular Physical Activity: Women engaged in regular physical activity may have higher protein needs to support muscle recovery and adaptation. Adjust protein intake based on individual responses and activity levels.

Choosing Protein Sources:

Variety of Protein Sources:

- Animal and Plant-Based Options: Incorporate a variety of protein sources, including both animal and plant-based options. This ensures a diverse amino acid profile and provides essential nutrients from different food groups.

Complete Proteins:

- Animal Proteins: Animal-based proteins are often complete, containing all essential amino acids. Include sources such as lean meats, poultry, fish, eggs, and dairy for comprehensive amino acid intake.

Combining Plant Proteins:

- Plant Proteins: If relying on plant-based sources, combine different plant proteins to achieve a more complete amino acid profile. Combinations such as beans and rice or tofu and quinoa provide complementary amino acids.

Timing of Protein Consumption:

Distribution Throughout the Day:

- Optimal Timing: Distribute protein intake throughout the day to support continuous muscle protein synthesis. Aim for balanced protein servings in meals and snacks to maximize the utilization of amino acids.

Post-Exercise Protein:

- Muscle Recovery: Consume protein after exercise to support muscle recovery. This post-exercise window is a critical time for protein intake to enhance muscle protein synthesis and repair.

Monitoring and Adjustments:

Regular Assessment:

- Response to Protein Intake: Regularly assess how your body responds to varying protein intake levels. Monitor changes in muscle mass, strength, and overall well-being to make informed adjustments.

Professional Guidance:

- Consultation with Experts: Seek guidance from nutritionists, dietitians, or fitness professionals for personalized advice on optimizing protein intake. Professional input can help align protein consumption with individual goals and health considerations.

Fat Consumption and Energy Levels: Balancing Your Ketogenic Lifestyle

In this subsection, we explore the crucial role of fat consumption in the ketogenic lifestyle and how it contributes to sustained energy levels. Understanding how to balance fat intake ensures optimal energy utilization and overall well-being within the ketogenic framework.

Role of Fat in Ketogenic Living:

Primary Energy Source:

- Fat as a Fuel: In the ketogenic lifestyle, fat serves as the primary energy source. When carbohydrates are restricted, the body enters ketosis, utilizing fats for energy production through the formation of ketone bodies.

Sustained Energy:

- Stable Energy Levels: Consuming an adequate amount of dietary fat provides a sustained and stable energy source. Fats are efficiently converted into ketones, which fuel various bodily functions, including the brain and muscles.

Customizing Fat Intake:

Individualized Needs:

- Energy Requirements: Customize your fat intake based on individual energy requirements, activity levels, and overall goals. Those with higher energy demands, such as athletes, may benefit from slightly higher fat intake.

Metabolic Adaptation:

- Adapting to Fat Metabolism: Allow time for the body to adapt to fat metabolism. During this adaptation phase, some individuals may experience variations in energy levels. Gradually increasing fat intake helps the body transition into ketosis more smoothly.

Quality of Dietary Fats:

Healthy Fat Sources:

- Prioritizing Healthy Fats: Emphasize sources of healthy fats to support overall well-being. Include monounsaturated fats (e.g., avocados, olive oil), polyunsaturated fats (e.g., fatty fish, nuts, seeds), and saturated fats from quality sources.

Omega-3 Fatty Acids:

- Balancing Omega-3s: Incorporate omega-3 fatty acids for their anti-inflammatory properties. Sources such as fatty fish, flaxseeds, and chia seeds contribute to a balanced omega-3 to omega-6 ratio.

Energy Levels and Satiety:

Fat for Sustained Energy:

● Satiety and Energy Stability: Fat-rich meals contribute to a sense of satiety and stable energy levels. Including sufficient fats in your diet helps prevent energy crashes and supports prolonged periods of sustained activity.

Combining Fats with Protein:

● Optimal Nutrient Combination: Combine fats with protein for balanced nutrient intake. Meals that include both fats and protein contribute to a satisfying and energy-sustaining eating experience.

Adjusting Fat Ratios:

Individual Responses:

● Monitoring Energy Levels: Regularly monitor how your body responds to varying fat ratios. Adjust fat intake based on individual preferences, energy levels, and overall well-being.

Fine-Tuning for Goals:

● Weight Management Goals: Fine-tune fat ratios based on specific weight management goals. While higher fat ratios are often associated with weight loss, adjustments may be made for those seeking weight maintenance or muscle gain.

Hydration and Electrolyte Balance:

Hydration Importance:

● Hydration and Energy: Ensure proper hydration to complement fat metabolism. Hydration supports the body's ability to efficiently utilize fats for energy production.

Electrolyte Management:

● Balancing Electrolytes: Maintain electrolyte balance, especially during the adaptation phase. Adequate sodium, potassium, magnesium, and calcium intake supports energy levels and mitigates potential side effects like fatigue.

Professional Guidance:

Consultation with Experts:

● Nutritional Guidance: Seek advice from nutritionists, dietitians, or healthcare professionals. Professional input can assist in customizing fat intake based on individual needs and health considerations.

Monitoring and Adjustments:

● Individual Responses: Regularly assess how your body responds to varying fat intake levels. Monitor changes in energy levels, satiety, and overall well-being to make informed adjustments.

Special Considerations for Hormonal Health: Nurturing Balance in Ketogenic Living

In this subsection, we explore special considerations for hormonal health within the ketogenic lifestyle. Understanding how the ketogenic diet may impact hormonal balance and implementing strategies to support women's health is crucial for overall well-being.

Hormonal Health and Ketogenic Living:

Potential Impact on Hormones:

- Hormonal Considerations: The ketogenic diet may influence hormonal balance, particularly for women. Awareness of potential impacts on menstrual cycles, reproductive health, and overall hormonal well-being is essential.

Individual Responses:

- Variability in Responses: Recognize that individual responses to the ketogenic diet can vary. Some women may experience changes in menstrual regularity, while others may not observe significant effects. Monitoring individual responses is key.

Balancing Hormones in Ketogenic Lifestyle:

Menstrual Cycle Awareness:

- Observing Menstrual Changes: Be attentive to changes in menstrual regularity, cycle length, or symptoms. Some women may experience alterations in the menstrual cycle during the initial stages of ketogenic adaptation.

Nutrient-Dense Choices:

- Supporting Hormonal Health: Prioritize nutrient-dense food choices to support hormonal balance. Include a variety of colorful vegetables, leafy greens, and berries to provide essential vitamins, minerals, and antioxidants.

Customizing Macronutrient Ratios:

Flexible Approach:

- Adjusting Ratios for Hormonal Balance: Consider a flexible approach to macronutrient ratios to support hormonal balance. Some women may benefit from slightly higher carbohydrate intake or variations in fat and protein ratios during different phases of the menstrual cycle.

Protein Intake for Women:

● Protein and Hormonal Support: Ensure adequate protein intake to support hormonal function. Protein-rich foods contribute to the production of hormones and provide essential amino acids for overall well-being.

Omega-3 Fatty Acids:

Importance of Omega-3s:

● Hormonal Benefits: Emphasize omega-3 fatty acids for their potential hormonal benefits. Sources such as fatty fish, flaxseeds, and chia seeds contribute to a balanced intake of essential fatty acids.

Balancing Omega-3 to Omega-6 Ratio:

● Anti-Inflammatory Support: Maintain a balanced omega-3 to omega-6 fatty acid ratio to support anti-inflammatory effects. Reducing the intake of processed oils high in omega-6 can contribute to a more favorable balance.

Hydration and Electrolyte Balance:

Addressing Hormonal Fluctuations:

● Hydration Strategies: Prioritize hydration to address potential hormonal fluctuations. Proper hydration supports overall well-being and can mitigate symptoms associated with hormonal changes.

Electrolyte Management:

● Balancing Electrolytes: Pay attention to electrolyte balance, especially during menstrual phases. Adequate intake of sodium, potassium, magnesium, and calcium helps maintain balance and supports hormonal health.

Consultation with Healthcare Professionals:

Individualized Guidance:

● Healthcare Professionals' Input: Seek advice from healthcare professionals, such as nutritionists or healthcare providers, for individualized guidance. Professional input is valuable for addressing specific hormonal concerns and optimizing overall well-being.

Monitoring and Adjustments:

● Observing Individual Responses: Regularly monitor individual responses to the ketogenic lifestyle. Pay attention to energy levels, mood, and hormonal changes, and make adjustments based on feedback and healthcare professional advice.

Impact on Thyroid Function: Navigating Thyroid Health in Ketogenic Living

In this subsection, we explore the potential impact of the ketogenic lifestyle on thyroid function and strategies to support thyroid health. Understanding how the ketogenic diet may influence the thyroid is essential for overall well-being.

Thyroid Function and Ketogenic Living:

Metabolic Effects of Ketogenic Diet:

- Influence on Metabolism: The ketogenic diet may influence metabolism, potentially affecting thyroid function. While some individuals experience positive outcomes, it's crucial to be aware of potential impacts on thyroid hormones.

Individual Variability:

- Responses Vary: Responses to the ketogenic diet can vary among individuals, and some may experience changes in thyroid markers. Monitoring thyroid function is important, especially for those with existing thyroid conditions.

Strategies to Support Thyroid Health:

Nutrient-Dense Choices:

- Thyroid-Supportive Nutrients: Prioritize nutrient-dense foods that support thyroid health. Include sources of iodine (e.g., seaweed, fish), selenium (e.g., Brazil nuts, poultry), and zinc (e.g., meat, nuts) in your ketogenic diet.

Adequate Caloric Intake:

- Avoiding Caloric Restriction: Avoid severe caloric restriction, as it may impact thyroid function. Ensure that your ketogenic approach supports adequate caloric intake to meet energy needs and prevent potential negative effects on the thyroid.

Monitoring and Adjustments:

Regular Thyroid Function Tests:

- Thyroid Panel Monitoring: Regularly monitor thyroid function through comprehensive thyroid panels. This includes assessments of TSH (thyroid-stimulating hormone), T3 (triiodothyronine), and T4 (thyroxine) levels.

Professional Guidance:

- Consultation with Healthcare Professionals: Seek guidance from healthcare professionals, especially if you have a pre-existing thyroid condition. Healthcare providers can offer individualized advice and monitor thyroid function based on your specific needs.

Balancing Macronutrient Ratios:

Moderation in Carbohydrate Restriction:

● Avoiding Extreme Carbohydrate Restriction: Avoid extreme carbohydrate restriction, as very low carbohydrate intake may impact thyroid function for some individuals. A moderate approach to carbohydrate intake can be considered.

Healthy Fat Choices:

● Balanced Fat Intake: Choose healthy fats that support overall health, including thyroid function. Include sources of monounsaturated fats (e.g., avocados, olive oil) and polyunsaturated fats (e.g., fatty fish, nuts) in your ketogenic diet.

Supplementation Considerations:

Iodine and Selenium Supplementation:

● Caution in Supplementation: Exercise caution when considering iodine and selenium supplementation. While these nutrients are essential for thyroid health, excessive intake can have adverse effects. Consult with healthcare professionals before supplementing.

Vitamin and Mineral Support:

● Comprehensive Nutrient Intake: Ensure comprehensive nutrient intake through a varied diet. A range of vitamins and minerals, including vitamin D, iron, and B-vitamins, supports overall health and may indirectly influence thyroid function.

Hydration and Electrolyte Balance:

Hydration Importance:

● Hydration and Thyroid Function: Prioritize hydration, as it plays a role in overall metabolic function, including thyroid health. Proper hydration supports optimal physiological processes.

Electrolyte Management:

● Balancing Electrolytes: Maintain electrolyte balance to support overall well-being. Adequate intake of sodium, potassium, magnesium, and calcium contributes to a balanced internal environment.

Individualized Approach:

Monitoring Personal Responses:

● Observing Thyroid Changes: Pay attention to individual responses and any changes in thyroid function. If you observe alterations in thyroid markers or experience symptoms, consult with healthcare professionals for guidance.

Customizing Ketogenic Approach:

● Tailoring to Individual Needs: Consider tailoring your ketogenic approach based on individual responses and health considerations. A personalized approach takes into account the dynamic nature of thyroid health.

Managing Menopausal Symptoms: Ketogenic Strategies for Women's Health

In this subsection, we explore strategies within the ketogenic lifestyle to manage menopausal symptoms and support women's health during this life stage. Understanding how dietary choices and lifestyle practices can positively impact menopausal experiences is essential for overall well-being.

Menopause and Ketogenic Living:

Hormonal Changes During Menopause:

- Impact on Hormones: Menopause is marked by hormonal changes, including a decline in estrogen levels. The ketogenic lifestyle offers strategies to manage symptoms associated with these hormonal shifts.

Symptom Management through Nutrition:

1. Nutrient-Dense Foods:

- Essential Vitamins and Minerals: Prioritize nutrient-dense foods rich in essential vitamins and minerals. A variety of colorful vegetables, leafy greens, and lean proteins contribute to overall well-being during menopause.

2. Omega-3 Fatty Acids:

- Anti-Inflammatory Support: Emphasize omega-3 fatty acids for their anti-inflammatory properties. Sources such as fatty fish, flaxseeds, and chia seeds may help manage inflammation and support joint health.

3. Healthy Fats for Brain Health:

- Cognitive Support: Include healthy fats, such as avocados and nuts, to support brain health. Omega-3 fatty acids and monounsaturated fats contribute to cognitive function, which may be beneficial during menopausal changes.

Balancing Macronutrient Ratios:

1. Sufficient Protein Intake:

- Muscle Maintenance: Ensure sufficient protein intake to support muscle maintenance. Protein-rich foods aid in preserving lean muscle mass, which can be especially important during menopause.

2. Customizing Fat Ratios:

- Individual Responses: Experiment with fat ratios based on individual responses. Some women find that a slightly higher fat intake contributes to satiety and energy levels during menopause.

3. Carbohydrate Moderation:

● **Blood Sugar Stability:** Moderate carbohydrate intake to promote stable blood sugar levels. This can help manage mood swings and energy fluctuations commonly associated with hormonal changes.

Physical Activity and Hormonal Balance:

1. Regular Exercise:

● **Endorphin Release:** Engage in regular exercise to release endorphins, which can positively impact mood and alleviate stress. Both cardiovascular and strength training exercises contribute to overall well-being.

2. Stress Management:

● **Mind-Body Practices:** Incorporate stress-reducing practices such as yoga, meditation, or deep-breathing exercises. Managing stress is crucial during menopause, as it can impact hormonal balance.

Hydration and Electrolyte Balance:

1. Optimal Hydration:

● **Hot Flash Management:** Stay optimally hydrated, as dehydration can exacerbate symptoms like hot flashes. Ensure a consistent intake of water and electrolyte-rich beverages.

2. Electrolyte Support:

● **Minimizing Fluid Retention:** Maintain electrolyte balance to minimize fluid retention. Adequate sodium, potassium, magnesium, and calcium intake can contribute to overall hydration and well-being.

Consultation with Healthcare Professionals:

1. Hormonal Health Checkups:

● **Regular Monitoring:** Undergo regular checkups with healthcare professionals to monitor hormonal health. Discuss any specific symptoms or concerns related to menopause for personalized guidance.

2. Individualized Approaches:

● **Tailored Recommendations:** Seek individualized recommendations for managing menopausal symptoms. Healthcare providers can offer insights into hormone replacement therapy or other interventions based on your health status.

Adapting to Individual Needs:

1. Personalized Strategies:

● **Trial and Observation:** Experiment with different ketogenic strategies and observe how your body responds. Personalized adjustments can enhance the effectiveness of the ketogenic lifestyle during menopause.

2. Mental and Emotional Well-being:

- Self-Care Practices: Prioritize mental and emotional well-being through self-care practices. Adequate sleep, social connections, and activities that bring joy contribute to overall health during menopause.

Meal Planning and Recipes: Crafting Delicious and Nutrient-Dense Ketogenic Meals

In this section, we delve into the art of meal planning and provide a collection of delicious and nutrient-dense ketogenic recipes. Meal planning is a key aspect of successful ketogenic living, ensuring that your dietary choices align with your health goals and preferences.

Meal Planning Strategies:

1. Macronutrient Considerations:

- Balancing Ratios: Plan meals that adhere to your desired macronutrient ratios. Balancing fats, proteins, and carbohydrates in a way that suits your individual goals and preferences is fundamental to ketogenic living.

2. Variety of Whole Foods:

- Colorful Plate: Incorporate a variety of whole foods to create a colorful and nutrient-rich plate. Include an array of vegetables, lean proteins, and healthy fats to ensure a diverse range of vitamins and minerals.

3. Portion Control:

- Mindful Portions: Practice portion control to align with your caloric and macronutrient goals. Being mindful of portion sizes can help prevent overeating and support weight management.

4. Timing of Meals:

- Meal Timing: Consider the timing of meals to support your daily schedule and energy needs. Some individuals may prefer intermittent fasting, while others may benefit from more frequent, smaller meals.

5. Hydration:

- Hydrate Strategically: Integrate hydration into your meal planning. Water-rich foods like cucumbers and watermelon can contribute to overall hydration, complementing your fluid intake.

Recipes for Ketogenic Living:

1. Avocado and Bacon Egg Cups:

- Ingredients:

Avocados

Eggs

Bacon

Salt and pepper to taste

● Instructions:

Preheat the oven to 375°F (190°C).

Cut avocados in half and remove the pits.

Scoop out some flesh to make room for the egg.

Place avocado halves in a baking dish.

Crack an egg into each avocado half.

Wrap each avocado half with a slice of bacon.

Season with salt and pepper.

Bake for 15-20 minutes or until eggs are cooked to your liking.

2. Salmon and Avocado Salad:

● Ingredients:

Grilled salmon fillets

Avocado, sliced

Mixed greens

Cherry tomatoes, halved

Olive oil, and lemon dressing

● Instructions:

Grill salmon fillets until cooked.

In a bowl, combine mixed greens, avocado slices, and cherry tomatoes.

Place grilled salmon on top.

Drizzle with olive oil and lemon dressing.

3. Cauliflower and Broccoli Mash:

● Ingredients:

Cauliflower florets

Broccoli florets

Butter

Salt and pepper to taste

- Instructions:

Steam cauliflower and broccoli until tender.

Mash together with butter.

Season with salt and pepper.

4. Zucchini Noodles with Pesto:

- Ingredients:

Zucchini noodles

Homemade or store-bought pesto

Cherry tomatoes, halved

Grated Parmesan cheese

- Instructions:

Sauté zucchini noodles until tender.

Toss with pesto and cherry tomatoes.

Sprinkle with grated Parmesan cheese.

5. Keto-friendly Chocolate Avocado Mousse:

- Ingredients:

Ripe avocados

Unsweetened cocoa powder

Coconut milk

Keto-friendly sweetener (e.g., erythritol)

Vanilla extract

- Instructions:

Blend avocados, cocoa powder, coconut milk, sweetener, and vanilla extract until smooth.

Chill in the refrigerator for a few hours before serving.

Customizing Recipes:

1. Flavor Enhancements:

● Herbs and Spices: Experiment with herbs and spices to enhance flavor without adding carbs. Fresh herbs, garlic, and spices like cumin or paprika can elevate your dishes.

2. Nut and Seed Variations:

● Texture and Nutrients: Incorporate different nuts and seeds for added texture and nutrients. Almonds, walnuts, chia seeds, or flaxseeds can contribute to both flavor and nutritional content.

3. Dairy or Non-Dairy Options:

● Dairy Substitutes: Consider dairy or non-dairy options based on your preferences. Almond milk, coconut milk, or dairy alternatives can be used in recipes that call for milk or cream.

4. Protein Choices:

● Diverse Proteins: Explore a variety of protein sources. Include fish, poultry, red meat, and plant-based proteins like tofu or tempeh to diversify your nutrient intake.

5. Creative Low-Carb Swaps:

● Alternative Ingredients: Get creative with low-carb swaps. Cauliflower rice, zucchini noodles, and almond flour are versatile alternatives in various recipes.

Creating Balanced Ketogenic Meals: Nourishing Your Body with Precision

In this section, we focus on the art of creating balanced ketogenic meals that nourish your body with precision. Achieving optimal macronutrient ratios and incorporating a variety of nutrient-dense foods ensures that each meal contributes to your overall well-being within the ketogenic lifestyle.

Key Principles of Balanced Ketogenic Meals:

1. Macronutrient Ratios:

- Balancing Fats, Proteins, and Carbs: Pay attention to the balance of fats, proteins, and carbohydrates in each meal. Strive to maintain your desired macronutrient ratios to support ketosis and your individual health goals.

2. Nutrient Density:

- Diverse and Colorful Plate: Aim for a diverse and colorful plate by including a variety of vegetables, leafy greens, and high-quality proteins. Nutrient-dense foods provide essential vitamins, minerals, and antioxidants crucial for overall well-being.

3. Portion Control:

- Mindful Portions: Practice mindful portion control to prevent overeating. Adjust portion sizes based on your caloric and macronutrient goals, ensuring that each meal aligns with your nutritional requirements.

4. Whole Foods Focus:

- Prioritizing Whole Foods: Emphasize whole, unprocessed foods in your meals. Whole foods provide a broad spectrum of nutrients and contribute to the overall quality of your ketogenic diet.

Sample Balanced Ketogenic Meals:

1. Grilled Salmon with Asparagus and Avocado:

- Ingredients:

Grilled salmon fillet

Asparagus spears

Sliced avocado

Olive oil drizzle

Lemon wedge

- Instructions:

Grill salmon until cooked.

Steam asparagus until tender.

Arrange salmon, asparagus, and sliced avocado on a plate.

Drizzle with olive oil and squeeze lemon over the top.

2. Chicken Caesar Salad with Parmesan Crisps:

- Ingredients:

Grilled chicken breast

Romaine lettuce

Caesar dressing (keto-friendly)

Parmesan crisps

- Instructions:

Grill chicken breast until cooked.

Toss grilled chicken with chopped romaine lettuce.

Drizzle with keto-friendly Caesar dressing.

Top with Parmesan crisps.

3. Beef and Broccoli Stir-Fry with Cauliflower Rice:

- Ingredients:

Thinly sliced beef strips

with Broccoli florets

Coconut aminos (soy sauce alternative)

Garlic and ginger

Cauliflower rice

- Instructions:

Stir-fry beef strips with broccoli, garlic, and ginger.

Add coconut aminos for flavor.

Serve over cauliflower rice.

4. Egg and Spinach Omelette with Avocado:

- Ingredients:

Eggs

Fresh spinach

Sliced avocado

Salt and pepper to taste

- Instructions:

Whisk eggs and pour into a hot pan.

Add fresh spinach and fold it into an omelette.

Season with salt and pepper.

Serve with sliced avocado on the side.

5. Zucchini Noodles with Pesto and Grilled Shrimp:

- Ingredients:

Zucchini noodles

Homemade or store-bought pesto

Grilled shrimp

Cherry tomatoes, halved

- Instructions:

Sauté zucchini noodles until tender.

Toss with pesto, grilled shrimp, and cherry tomatoes.

Serve with a sprinkle of Parmesan cheese.

Customizing for Personal Preferences:

1. Flavor Enhancements:

- Herbs and Spices: Experiment with herbs and spices to enhance flavor without adding carbs. Fresh herbs, garlic, and spices can elevate the taste of your meals.

2. Texture Variations:

- Nuts and Seeds: Include nuts and seeds for added texture and nutrients. Almonds, walnuts, or chia seeds can contribute to both flavor and nutritional content.

3. Sauce and Dressing Options:

- **Low-Carb Sauces:** Explore low-carb sauce and dressing options. Choose keto-friendly alternatives to traditional high-carb sauces to enhance the taste of your meals.

4. Creative Low-Carb Swaps:

- **Alternative Ingredients:** Get creative with low-carb swaps. Cauliflower rice, zucchini noodles, and almond flour are versatile alternatives in various recipes.

5. Seasonal and Local Produce:

- **Fresh and Seasonal Choices:** Incorporate fresh and seasonal produce. Opting for local and seasonal ingredients not only enhances flavor but also supports sustainability.

Building a Nutrient-Dense Plate: Precision in Ketogenic Nourishment

In this section, we delve into the meticulous process of building a nutrient-dense plate within the ketogenic framework. By strategically selecting a variety of high-quality foods, you can ensure that each plate contributes to your overall well-being and aligns with the principles of the ketogenic lifestyle.

Foundations of a Nutrient-Dense Plate:

1. Quality Protein Source:

- **Lean and Fatty Proteins:** Include a quality protein source in each meal. Opt for a variety of lean and fatty proteins such as poultry, fish, beef, eggs, or plant-based proteins like tofu or tempeh.

2. Abundant Vegetables and Greens:

- **Colorful Vegetable Variety:** Build your plate with an abundance of colorful vegetables and leafy greens. These provide essential vitamins, minerals, and antioxidants crucial for optimal health within the ketogenic lifestyle.

3. Healthy Fats:

- **Balanced Fat Choices:** Integrate healthy fats into your plate for satiety and energy. Choose sources such as avocados, olive oil, nuts, seeds, and fatty fish to contribute to your fat intake while maintaining a balance of omega-3 and omega-6 fatty acids.

4. Low-Carb, Non-Starchy Options:

- **Minimize Carbohydrates:** Keep carbohydrate content in check by selecting low-carb, non-starchy options. Cauliflower, broccoli, zucchini, and leafy greens are excellent choices to add bulk and nutrients without excessive carbs.

Building a Sample Nutrient-Dense Plate:

1. Grilled Chicken Caesar Salad:

- Components:

Grilled chicken breast

Romaine lettuce

Cherry tomatoes

Cucumber slices

Avocado slices

Parmesan crisps

Caesar dressing (keto-friendly)

- Assembly:

Grill chicken breast and slice into strips.

Arrange a bed of romaine lettuce on the plate.

Scatter cherry tomatoes, cucumber slices, and avocado slices.

Top with grilled chicken strips.

Sprinkle Parmesan crisps for added texture.

Drizzle with keto-friendly Caesar dressing.

2. Salmon and Broccoli with Almond Butter Sauce:

- Components:

Grilled salmon fillet

Steamed broccoli florets

Almond butter sauce (almond butter, coconut aminos, garlic)

- Assembly:

Grill salmon until cooked.

Steam broccoli until tender.

Place salmon on the plate with a side of steamed broccoli.

Drizzle with almond butter sauce.

3. Zucchini Noodle Stir-Fry with Tofu:

- Components:

Zucchini noodles

Tofu cubes

Bell peppers (assorted colors)

Snow peas

Sesame oil and soy sauce (keto-friendly)

- Assembly:

Sauté tofu cubes until golden.

Stir-fry zucchini noodles, bell peppers, and snow peas.

Combine sautéed tofu with the vegetable stir-fry.

Drizzle with a mixture of sesame oil and keto-friendly soy sauce.

4. Avocado and Shrimp Salad Bowl:

- Components:

Avocado slices

Grilled shrimp

Mixed greens

Radishes, sliced

Cilantro leaves

Lime wedges

- Assembly:

Grill shrimp until cooked.

Arrange mixed greens on the plate.

Scatter avocado slices, radish slices, and grilled shrimp.

Garnish with fresh cilantro leaves.

Serve with lime wedges for added flavor.

Customization and Flavor Enhancements:

1. Nut and Seed Toppings:

- Crunchy Additions: Sprinkle nuts or seeds for added crunch and nutritional content. Almonds, walnuts, or chia seeds can complement the texture of your plate.

2. Herbs and Spices:

- Flavorful Garnishes: Use fresh herbs and spices as flavorful garnishes. Parsley, basil, cilantro, or a sprinkle of your favorite spice blend can elevate the taste of your meal.

3. Low-Carb Sauce Options:

- Sauce Varieties: Experiment with low-carb sauce options to enhance flavor. Whether it's a garlic butter sauce, a lemon vinaigrette, or a keto-friendly teriyaki, choose options that align with your preferences.

4. Seasonal and Local Choices:

- Fresh and Seasonal Ingredients: Incorporate fresh and seasonal produce for variety and flavor. Opting for local and seasonal ingredients supports sustainability and provides a range of nutrients.

5. Creative Low-Carb Swaps:

- Alternative Ingredients: Get creative with low-carb swaps to recreate classic dishes. Cauliflower rice, zucchini noodles, or almond flour can be versatile substitutes.

Meal Timing and Frequency: Crafting an Optimal Eating Schedule within Ketogenic Living

In this section, we explore the significance of meal timing and frequency within the context of ketogenic living. Crafting an optimal eating schedule plays a crucial role in supporting ketosis, energy levels, and overall well-being. Understanding the principles of meal timing can enhance the effectiveness of your ketogenic lifestyle.

Key Considerations for Meal Timing:

1. Intermittent Fasting Strategies:

- Periods of Fasting: Explore intermittent fasting strategies within the ketogenic lifestyle. This approach involves cycling between periods of eating and fasting, promoting fat-burning and metabolic flexibility.

2. Personalized Eating Windows:

- Adaptation to Preferences: Customize your eating windows based on personal preferences and daily routines. Whether you prefer a shorter daily eating window or intermittent fasting on specific days, tailor the approach to suit your lifestyle.

3. Fueling Workouts:

- Pre-Workout Nutrition: Consider the timing of meals concerning workouts. Some individuals benefit from a pre-workout meal to provide energy, while others prefer exercising in a fasted state. Experiment with both approaches to determine what works best for you.

4. Consistency in Timing:

- Establishing Consistency: Aim for consistency in meal timing to support metabolic regulation. Establishing regular eating patterns can contribute to stable blood sugar levels and optimize energy throughout the day.

5. Listen to Hunger Signals:

- Intuitive Eating: Pay attention to hunger signals and practice intuitive eating. Allow your body's natural cues to guide meal timing, helping you align with your nutritional needs without strict adherence to a predetermined schedule.

Meal Frequency Strategies:

1. Traditional Three Meals:

- Balanced Distribution: Follow a traditional three-meal-a-day approach with balanced macronutrient distribution. Ensure that each meal contains an appropriate balance of fats, proteins, and carbohydrates to support ketosis.

2. Two Meals and a Snack:

- Snacking Moderation: Consider a two-meal-a-day structure with a small snack if needed. This approach can provide sufficient time for fasting periods while allowing for nutrient intake during the eating windows.

3. One Meal a Day (OMAD):

- Extended Fasting Period: Explore the One Meal a Day (OMAD) approach for an extended fasting period. This involves consuming all daily calories within a single meal, allowing for an extended fasting window.

4. Cyclical Ketogenic Approach:

- Strategic Carbohydrate Intake: Implement a cyclical ketogenic approach, incorporating periods of higher carbohydrate intake strategically. This can be beneficial for athletes or individuals with specific performance goals.

5. Seasonal or Occasional Fasting:

- Variability in Frequency: Introduce seasonal or occasional fasting for variability. Periods of longer fasts, such as 24 hours or more, can be practiced intermittently for potential metabolic benefits.

Optimizing Meal Timing for Ketogenic Living:

1. Assessing Individual Response:

- Observation and Adjustment: Monitor your individual response to different meal timing strategies. Pay attention to energy levels, ketone production, and overall well-being, adjusting your approach based on personal observations.

2. Professional Guidance:

- Consultation with Healthcare Professionals: Seek guidance from healthcare professionals, especially if you have specific health conditions or concerns. Healthcare providers can offer personalized advice on meal timing that aligns with your health goals.

3. Lifestyle Adaptation:

- Integration with Lifestyle: Tailor meal timing to integrate seamlessly with your lifestyle. Consider work schedules, family routines, and personal preferences to create an eating schedule that supports long-term adherence.

4. Experimentation and Flexibility:

- Dynamic Approach: Approach meal timing with a spirit of experimentation and flexibility. Your optimal eating schedule may evolve over time, and being open to adjustments can contribute to a sustainable ketogenic lifestyle.

5. Mindful Eating Practices:

- Savoring Meals: Practice mindful eating to enhance the enjoyment and satisfaction of meals. Pay attention to the sensory experience, savor flavors, and be present during mealtime for a holistic approach to nourishment.

Sample Meal Plans for Women: A Week of Nourishing Ketogenic Delights

In this section, we present a week of sample meal plans designed specifically for women following a ketogenic lifestyle. These meal plans are crafted to provide balanced nutrition, support ketosis, and cater to the unique nutritional needs of women. Feel free to customize these plans based on individual preferences and dietary requirements.

Note: Adjust portion sizes and macronutrient ratios based on personal goals and caloric needs.

Day 1: Balanced Ketogenic Day

Breakfast:

- Scrambled eggs with spinach cooked in butter

- Avocado slices

- Bulletproof coffee (coffee with MCT oil and unsalted butter)

Lunch:

- Grilled chicken Caesar salad with keto-friendly dressing

- Parmesan crisps

Snack:

- Handful of macadamia nuts

Dinner:

- Baked salmon fillet with lemon and herbs

- Steamed broccoli with butter

- Mixed green salad with olive oil dressing

Day 2: Intermittent Fasting Day

Morning:

- Black coffee or herbal tea

Late Morning (Breakfast):

- Keto-friendly smoothie with unsweetened almond milk, spinach, and protein powder

Afternoon (Lunch):

- Cobb salad with grilled chicken, bacon, avocado, and blue cheese dressing

Snack:

- Celery sticks with cream cheese

Evening (Dinner):

- Zucchini noodle stir-fry with shrimp, broccoli, and soy sauce

- Side of cauliflower rice

Day 3: One Meal a Day (OMAD) Approach

OMAD Dinner:

- Ribeye steak cooked in olive oil

- Roasted Brussels sprouts with garlic

- Caesar salad with extra-virgin olive oil dressing

Snack (if needed):

- Full-fat Greek yogurt with a few raspberries

Day 4: Cyclical Ketogenic Day

Breakfast:

- Keto pancakes made with almond flour, served with sugar-free syrup

- Scrambled eggs with cheese

Lunch:

- Turkey and avocado lettuce wraps with mayonnaise

- Side of cherry tomatoes

Snack:

- Greek salad with feta cheese, olives, and olive oil dressing

Dinner:

- Grilled salmon with dill sauce

- Asparagus spears sautéed in butter

- Cauliflower mash with cream and chives

Day 5: Two Meals and a Snack

Breakfast:

- Omelette with mushrooms, cheese, and spinach

- Sliced strawberries

Lunch:

- Chicken and vegetable skewers grilled with olive oil

- Mixed greens salad with avocado and balsamic vinaigrette

Snack:

- Handful of almonds and walnuts

Dinner:

- Baked cod fillets with lemon and herbs

- Zucchini noodles sautéed in garlic butter

Day 6: Balanced Ketogenic Day

Breakfast:

- Greek yogurt parfait with berries and crushed nuts

Lunch:

- Shrimp and avocado salad with mixed greens

- Caesar dressing with extra-virgin olive oil

Snack:

- Celery sticks with almond butter

Dinner:

- Beef stir-fry with broccoli, bell peppers, and sesame oil

- Side of cauliflower rice

Day 7: Flexibility Day

Adapt meals based on preferences and leftovers:

- Choose from a variety of keto-friendly recipes, incorporating your favorite proteins, vegetables, and fats.

Snacks:

- Cheese cubes, olives, or pork rinds

Hydration:

- Emphasize water, herbal teas, or flavored water with electrolytes throughout the day.

These sample meal plans offer a variety of delicious and nutrient-dense options for women following a ketogenic lifestyle. Remember to listen to your body's hunger and satiety signals, stay hydrated, and adjust portion sizes based on individual needs.

Daily and Weekly Meal Plans: Tailoring Your Ketogenic Journey

In this section, we provide daily and weekly meal plans that can be tailored to support your ketogenic lifestyle. These plans offer variety, balance, and flexibility to accommodate individual preferences and nutritional needs. Feel free to adjust portion sizes and substitute ingredients based on personal preferences and dietary requirements.

Note: Customize these plans based on your specific caloric and macronutrient goals.

Daily Meal Plan: Balanced Ketogenic Day

Breakfast:

- Scrambled eggs with spinach and feta cheese

- Sliced avocado

- Bulletproof coffee (coffee with MCT oil and unsalted butter)

Lunch:

- Grilled chicken salad with mixed greens, cherry tomatoes, and ranch dressing

- Parmesan crisps

Snack:

- Handful of almonds and walnuts

Dinner:

- Baked salmon with lemon and dill

- Steamed broccoli with butter

- Cauliflower mash with cream and chives

Daily Meal Plan: Intermittent Fasting Day

Morning:

- Black coffee or herbal tea

Late Morning (Breakfast):

- Keto-friendly smoothie with unsweetened almond milk, spinach, and protein powder

Afternoon (Lunch):

- Cobb salad with grilled chicken, bacon, avocado, and blue cheese dressing

Snack:

- Celery sticks with cream cheese

Evening (Dinner):

- Zucchini noodle stir-fry with shrimp, broccoli, and soy sauce
- Side of cauliflower rice

Daily Meal Plan: One Meal a Day (OMAD) Approach

OMAD Dinner:

- Ribeye steak cooked in olive oil
- Roasted Brussels sprouts with garlic
- Caesar salad with extra-virgin olive oil dressing

Snack (if needed):

- Full-fat Greek yogurt with a few raspberries

Daily Meal Plan: Cyclical Ketogenic Day

Breakfast:

- Keto pancakes made with almond flour, served with sugar-free syrup
- Scrambled eggs with cheese

Lunch:

- Turkey and avocado lettuce wraps with mayonnaise
- Side of cherry tomatoes

Snack:

- Greek salad with feta cheese, olives, and olive oil dressing

Dinner:

- Grilled salmon with dill sauce

- Asparagus spears sautéed in butter

- Cauliflower mash with cream and chives

Weekly Meal Plan: Two Meals and a Snack Day

Day 1:

- Breakfast: Omelette with mushrooms, cheese, and spinach

- Lunch: Chicken and vegetable skewers grilled with olive oil

- Snack: Handful of almonds and walnuts

- Dinner: Baked cod fillets with lemon and herbs, zucchini noodles sautéed in garlic butter

Day 2:

- Breakfast: Greek yogurt parfait with berries and crushed nuts

- Lunch: Shrimp and avocado salad with mixed greens, Caesar dressing with extra-virgin olive oil

- Snack: Celery sticks with almond butter

- Dinner: Beef stir-fry with broccoli, bell peppers, and sesame oil, side of cauliflower rice

Weekly Meal Plan: Flexibility Day

Adapt meals based on preferences and leftovers:

- Choose from a variety of keto-friendly recipes, incorporating your favorite proteins, vegetables, and fats.

Snacks:

- Cheese cubes, olives, or pork rinds

Hydration:

- Emphasize water, herbal teas, or flavored water with electrolytes throughout the day.

Adjusting for Dietary Preferences: Crafting a Ketogenic Lifestyle to Suit Your Tastes

In this section, we explore how to adjust ketogenic meal plans to accommodate various dietary preferences. Whether you follow vegetarian, pescatarian, or other specific dietary preferences, adapting your ketogenic approach ensures a personalized and enjoyable journey. Feel free to mix and match ingredients to create meals that align with your tastes and values.

Note: Adjust portion sizes based on individual caloric needs and nutritional goals.

Vegetarian Ketogenic Day:

Breakfast:

- Avocado and egg salad with cherry tomatoes

- Feta cheese crumbles

- Herbal tea with a splash of heavy cream

Lunch:

- Zucchini noodles with pesto sauce and pine nuts

- Grilled halloumi cheese

Snack:

- Celery sticks with cream cheese and sliced almonds

Dinner:

- Cauliflower crust pizza with tomato sauce, mozzarella cheese, and assorted vegetables

- Mixed green salad with avocado and olive oil dressing

Pescatarian Ketogenic Day:

Breakfast:

- Smoked salmon and cream cheese roll-ups

- Cucumber slices

- Bulletproof coffee with MCT oil

Lunch:

- Tuna salad lettuce wraps with mayonnaise

- Cherry tomatoes and olives

Snack:

- Seaweed snacks and a handful of macadamia nuts

Dinner:

- Grilled shrimp skewers with lemon and garlic butter

- Broccoli sautéed in olive oil

- Avocado and cherry tomato salad

Vegan Ketogenic Day:

Breakfast:

- Chia seed pudding made with unsweetened almond milk and topped with berries

- Almond butter drizzle

Lunch:

- Vegan keto stir-fry with tofu, broccoli, and bell peppers

- Cauliflower rice

Snack:

- Avocado slices with salt and pepper

Dinner:

- Eggplant lasagna with vegan cheese and tomato sauce

- Side of sautéed spinach in coconut oil

Dairy-Free Ketogenic Day:

Breakfast:

- Coconut milk smoothie with spinach, berries, and vegan protein powder

Lunch:

- Almond-crusted tofu salad with mixed greens and balsamic vinaigrette

- Avocado slices

Snack:

- Coconut yogurt with a sprinkle of unsweetened coconut flakes

Dinner:

- Stir-fried tempeh with broccoli, mushrooms, and sesame oil

- Cauliflower mash with coconut cream

Flexitarian Ketogenic Day:

Breakfast:

- Greek yogurt bowl with nuts, seeds, and a drizzle of honey

Lunch:

- Grilled chicken breast salad with mixed greens and vinaigrette dressing

- Feta cheese crumbles

Snack:

- Hummus with cucumber and bell pepper sticks

Dinner:

- Baked cod fillets with lemon and herbs

- Asparagus spears sautéed in olive oil

- Quinoa and kale salad with a lemon-tahini dressing

Nut-Free Ketogenic Day:

Breakfast:

- Coconut flour pancakes with sugar-free syrup

- Scrambled eggs with sautéed spinach

Lunch:

- Turkey and avocado lettuce wraps with mayonnaise

- Cherry tomatoes and olives

Snack:

- Sunflower seed butter with celery sticks

Dinner:

- Grilled salmon with dill sauce

- Zucchini noodles sautéed in avocado oil

- Mixed green salad with olive oil dressing

- Zucchini noodles sautéed in avocado oil

- Mixed green salad with olive oil dressing

Delicious Ketogenic Recipes: Culinary Delights for Your Ketogenic Journey

In this section, we present a collection of mouthwatering ketogenic recipes that showcase the diversity and flavor of ketogenic cuisine. These recipes are crafted to suit different tastes and preferences, providing a delightful culinary experience within the framework of a ketogenic lifestyle. Enjoy experimenting with these recipes and make them your own!

Note: Adjust portion sizes based on individual caloric needs and nutritional goals.

1. Avocado and Bacon Egg Cups:

Ingredients:

- Ripe avocados, halved and pitted

- Eggs

- Bacon strips

- Salt and pepper to taste

- Chopped chives for garnish

Instructions:

Preheat the oven to 375°F (190°C).

Place avocado halves in a baking dish.

Crack an egg into each avocado half.

Wrap each avocado with a bacon strip.

Season with salt and pepper.

Bake in the oven for 20-25 minutes or until the eggs are cooked to your liking.

Garnish with chopped chives before serving.

2. Lemon Garlic Butter Grilled Salmon:

Ingredients:

- Salmon fillets

- Lemon, sliced

- Garlic cloves, minced

- Butter, melted

- Fresh dill, chopped

- Salt and pepper to taste

Instructions:

Preheat the grill to medium-high heat.

Season salmon fillets with salt and pepper.

In a bowl, mix melted butter, minced garlic, and chopped dill.

Place salmon fillets on the grill, placing lemon slices on top.

Brush the salmon with the garlic butter mixture.

Grill for 10-12 minutes or until the salmon is cooked through.

Serve with additional lemon slices and garnish with fresh dill.

3. Cauliflower Fried Rice with Shrimp:

Ingredients:

- Cauliflower rice

- Shrimp, peeled and deveined

- Mixed vegetables (peas, carrots, bell peppers)

- Soy sauce (or coconut aminos for a soy-free option)

- Sesame oil

- Garlic, minced

- Green onions, chopped

- Salt and pepper to taste

Instructions:

In a large pan, sauté shrimp with minced garlic until cooked. Set aside.

In the same pan, stir-fry mixed vegetables until tender.

Add cauliflower rice and cook until it reaches your desired consistency.

Mix in cooked shrimp, soy sauce, and sesame oil.

Season with salt and pepper to taste.

Garnish with chopped green onions before serving.

4. Cheesy Bacon Wrapped Asparagus:

Ingredients:

- Fresh asparagus spears

- Bacon strips

- Cream cheese

- Shredded cheddar cheese

- Garlic powder

- Salt and pepper to taste

Instructions:

Preheat the oven to 400°F (200°C).

Trim the ends of asparagus spears.

Spread a thin layer of cream cheese on each bacon strip.

Wrap bacon around each asparagus spear.

Place the wrapped asparagus on a baking sheet.

Sprinkle shredded cheddar cheese, garlic powder, salt, and pepper.

Bake for 20-25 minutes or until the bacon is crispy.

5. Zucchini Noodle Alfredo with Chicken:

Ingredients:

- Zucchini noodles

- Grilled chicken breast, sliced

- Heavy cream

- Parmesan cheese, grated

- Garlic, minced

- Butter

- Salt and pepper to taste

- Fresh parsley, chopped

Instructions:

In a pan, melt butter and sauté minced garlic until fragrant.

Pour in heavy cream and bring to a simmer.

Stir in grated Parmesan cheese until the sauce thickens.

Season with salt and pepper to taste.

Add zucchini noodles and sliced grilled chicken to the sauce.

Toss until the noodles are coated and the chicken is heated through.

Garnish with chopped fresh parsley before serving.

Breakfast, Lunch, Dinner, and Snack Ideas: A Palette of Ketogenic Delights

In this section, we provide a variety of breakfast, lunch, dinner, and snack ideas to add vibrancy to your ketogenic lifestyle. These suggestions encompass diverse flavors and ingredients, allowing you to customize your meals based on preferences and nutritional needs. Feel free to mix and match ideas to create a personalized and enjoyable ketogenic menu.

Note: Adjust portion sizes based on individual caloric needs and nutritional goals.

Breakfast Ideas:

Egg Muffins:

- Ingredients: Eggs, spinach, feta cheese, cherry tomatoes.

- Instructions: Whisk eggs, mix with veggies and cheese, pour into muffin cups, and bake until set.

Chia Seed Pudding:

- Ingredients: Chia seeds, unsweetened almond milk, vanilla extract, berries.

- Instructions: Mix chia seeds with almond milk and vanilla, refrigerate overnight, and top with berries.

Keto Smoothie:

- Ingredients: Unsweetened almond milk, spinach, avocado, protein powder, chia seeds.

- Instructions: Blend all ingredients until smooth.

Keto Pancakes:

- Ingredients: Almond flour, eggs, almond milk, baking powder.

- Instructions: Mix ingredients, cook like pancakes, and top with sugar-free syrup.

Avocado and Bacon Egg Cups:

- Ingredients: Avocados, eggs, bacon, chives.

- Instructions: Bake halved avocados with eggs and bacon until eggs are set, garnish with chives.

Lunch Ideas:

Chicken Caesar Salad:

- Ingredients: Grilled chicken, romaine lettuce, Parmesan crisps, Caesar dressing.

- Instructions: Toss ingredients together, top with dressing and Parmesan crisps.

Zucchini Noodle Alfredo with Shrimp:

- Ingredients: Zucchini noodles, shrimp, Alfredo sauce.

- Instructions: Sauté shrimp, toss with zucchini noodles and Alfredo sauce.

Cobb Salad Wrap:

- Ingredients: Turkey slices, bacon, avocado, lettuce, blue cheese dressing.

- Instructions: Assemble ingredients in a low-carb wrap or lettuce leaves.

Tuna Salad Lettuce Wraps:

- Ingredients: Tuna, mayonnaise, celery, lettuce leaves.

- Instructions: Mix tuna with mayo and celery, and spoon into lettuce leaves.

Keto Stir-Fry:

- Ingredients: Beef strips, broccoli, bell peppers, soy sauce.

- Instructions: Stir-fry beef and veggies in soy sauce until cooked.

Dinner Ideas:

Grilled Salmon with Lemon and Dill:

- Ingredients: Salmon fillets, lemon, dill, garlic.

- Instructions: Grill salmon with lemon, dill, and garlic until cooked.

Beef and Broccoli Stir-Fry:

- Ingredients: Beef strips, broccoli, sesame oil, soy sauce.

- Instructions: Stir-fry beef and broccoli in sesame oil and soy sauce.

Eggplant Lasagna:

- Ingredients: Eggplant slices, tomato sauce, vegan cheese.

- Instructions: Layer eggplant slices with tomato sauce and vegan cheese, and bake until bubbly.

Cauliflower Crust Pizza:

- Ingredients: Cauliflower crust, tomato sauce, cheese, assorted toppings.

- Instructions: Top cauliflower crust with sauce, cheese, and desired toppings, and bake until golden.

Shrimp Scampi with Zucchini Noodles:

- Ingredients: Shrimp, zucchini noodles, garlic, lemon, butter.

- Instructions: Sauté shrimp with garlic, lemon, and butter, toss with zucchini noodles.

Snack Ideas:

Cheese and Pepperoni:

- Ingredients: Cheese cubes, pepperoni slices.

- Instructions: Enjoy cheese and pepperoni as a quick snack.

Guacamole with Veggie Sticks:

- Ingredients: Avocado, lime, tomato, onion, bell pepper sticks.

- Instructions: Mash avocado with lime, tomato, and onion, dip with bell pepper sticks.

Keto Trail Mix:

- Ingredients: Mixed nuts, seeds, dark chocolate.

- Instructions: Mix nuts, seeds, and dark chocolate for a satisfying trail mix.

Greek Yogurt Parfait:

- Ingredients: Greek yogurt, berries, crushed nuts.

- Instructions: Layer Greek yogurt with berries and crushed nuts for a parfait.

Deviled Eggs:

- Ingredients: Hard-boiled eggs, mayonnaise, mustard.

- Instructions: Mix egg yolks with mayo and mustard, and spoon back into egg whites.

Creative and Flavorful Ketogenic Cooking: Elevate Your Culinary Experience

In this section, we delve into the realm of creative and flavorful ketogenic cooking, exploring techniques, ingredients, and recipes that add excitement to your kitchen. Whether you're a seasoned chef or a novice cook, these ideas will inspire you to create delicious and satisfying ketogenic meals that go beyond the ordinary. Get ready to elevate your culinary experience and savor the richness of ketosis.

Note: Adjust portion sizes based on individual caloric needs and nutritional goals.

1. Herb-Infused Oils and Butter:

Ingredients:

- Extra-virgin olive oil or grass-fed butter
- Fresh herbs (rosemary, thyme, basil, oregano)
- Garlic cloves

Instructions:

Heat olive oil or butter in a pan over low heat.

Add fresh herbs and garlic cloves.

Infuse for 10-15 minutes, then strain.

Use herb-infused oils for drizzling over salads or dipping, and herb-infused butter for cooking or finishing meats.

2. Keto-Friendly Sauces and Dressings:

Ingredients:

- Avocado oil or olive oil
- Vinegar (apple cider vinegar, balsamic vinegar)
- Mustard (Dijon or whole grain)
- Fresh herbs (parsley, cilantro, dill)
- Garlic, minced
- Salt and pepper

Instructions:

Combine ingredients in a bowl and whisk until emulsified.

Adjust ratios for desired consistency and taste.

Use as a salad dressing, marinade, or sauce for meats and vegetables.

3. Stuffed Avocado Boats:

Ingredients:

- Ripe avocados, halved and pitted

- Protein of choice (chicken, shrimp, tuna)

- Vegetables (bell peppers, cherry tomatoes, onions)

- Cheese (feta, cheddar, or goat cheese)

- Fresh herbs (cilantro, parsley)

Instructions:

Scoop out some avocado to create a boat-like shape.

Mix protein, vegetables, cheese, and herbs in a bowl.

Fill avocado halves with the mixture.

Bake until cheese is melted and ingredients are heated through.

4. Cauliflower Rice Sushi Rolls:

Ingredients:

- Cauliflower rice

- Nori sheets

- Sliced avocado, cucumber, and fish of choice (salmon, tuna)

- Sesame seeds

- Soy sauce or coconut aminos

Instructions:

Lay a nori sheet on a bamboo rolling mat.

Spread a thin layer of cauliflower rice on the nori.

Add avocado, cucumber, and fish slices.

Roll tightly and slice into sushi rolls.

Serve with soy sauce or coconut aminos.

5. Keto-Friendly Zoodle Carbonara:

Ingredients:

- Zucchini noodles (zoodles)

- Bacon strips, chopped

- Eggs

- Parmesan cheese, grated

- Fresh parsley, chopped

- Garlic, minced

Instructions:

Sauté chopped bacon until crispy.

In a bowl, whisk eggs, grated Parmesan, minced garlic, and chopped parsley.

Cook zucchini noodles in the bacon fat.

Toss noodles with the egg mixture until creamy.

Mix in crispy bacon and serve.

6. Spiced Roasted Nuts:

Ingredients:

- Mixed nuts (almonds, walnuts, pecans)

- Olive oil

- Spices (cayenne pepper, paprika, garlic powder)

- Salt

Instructions:

Toss mixed nuts in olive oil.

Sprinkle with spices and salt to taste.

Roast in the oven until the nuts are golden and fragrant.

Allow to cool before serving as a flavorful snack.

7. Keto-Friendly Dessert Parfait:

Ingredients:

- Sugar-free whipped cream

- Berries (strawberries, blueberries, raspberries)

- Dark chocolate, grated or shaved

- Crushed nuts (almonds, walnuts)

- Unsweetened coconut flakes

Instructions:

Layer whipped cream, berries, grated chocolate, and crushed nuts in a glass.

Repeat layers until the glass is filled.

Top with unsweetened coconut flakes.

Chill before serving as a delightful ketogenic dessert.

8. Keto-Friendly Ice Cream:

Ingredients:

- Heavy cream

- Unsweetened almond milk

- Erythritol or stevia

- Vanilla extract

- Dark chocolate chips or nuts (optional)

Instructions:

Whip heavy cream until stiff peaks form.

In a separate bowl, mix almond milk, sweetener, and vanilla extract.

Gently fold the almond milk mixture into the whipped cream.

Add dark chocolate chips or nuts if desired.

Freeze until firm and enjoy keto-friendly ice cream.

Navigating Challenges: Overcoming Hurdles on Your Ketogenic Journey

In this section, we address common challenges that individuals may encounter on their ketogenic journey and provide strategies to overcome them. Navigating hurdles is an integral part of any lifestyle change, and with the right mindset and practical solutions, you can successfully navigate challenges and continue thriving within the ketogenic lifestyle.

1. Keto Flu and Electrolyte Imbalance:

Challenge:

- Some individuals may experience symptoms of the keto flu during the initial stages of transitioning to a ketogenic diet, including fatigue, headaches, and muscle cramps.

Solution:

- Stay hydrated and ensure an adequate intake of electrolytes (sodium, potassium, magnesium).

- Include electrolyte-rich foods such as leafy greens, avocados, and nuts.

- Consider taking electrolyte supplements if needed.

2. Social Situations and Dining Out:

Challenge:

- Social gatherings and dining out can present challenges in adhering to a ketogenic diet, with tempting high-carb options.

Solution:

- Plan by checking menus and making informed choices.

- Opt for keto-friendly options, such as salads, grilled meats, and non-starchy vegetables.

- Communicate dietary preferences with hosts or restaurant staff.

3. Plateau in Weight Loss:

Challenge:

- Some individuals may experience a plateau in weight loss, where progress slows down or halts.

Solution:

- Reevaluate portion sizes and caloric intake.

- Incorporate intermittent fasting or change meal timing.

- Increase physical activity or modify exercise routines.

4. Emotional Eating and Cravings:

Challenge:

- Emotional triggers and cravings for high-carb foods can be challenging to manage.

Solution:

- Practice mindfulness and identify emotional triggers.

- Choose satisfying keto-friendly alternatives for cravings.

- Seek support from friends, family, or a support group.

5. Traveling and Limited Food Options:

Challenge:

- Traveling may limit access to preferred keto-friendly foods, leading to potential deviations from the diet.

Solution:

- Pack keto-friendly snacks and meals for travel.

- Research local dining options or grocery stores at your destination.

- Choose high-fat, low-carb options when dining out.

6. Digestive Issues:

Challenge:

- Some individuals may experience digestive issues, such as constipation or diarrhea, when transitioning to a ketogenic diet.

Solution:

- Ensure an adequate intake of fiber through vegetables and low-carb sources.

- Stay hydrated and consider adding sources of healthy fats, such as avocados and olive oil.

7. Tracking and Monitoring Macros:

Challenge:

- Accurately tracking and monitoring macronutrient intake may be challenging for some individuals.

Solution:

- Use apps or tools to track macros and monitor nutritional intake.

- Plan meals in advance to meet macro goals.

- Seek guidance from a nutritionist or dietitian if needed.

8. Sustainability and Long-Term Commitment:

Challenge:

- Maintaining a ketogenic lifestyle over the long term may require ongoing commitment and dedication.

Solution:

- Focus on the health benefits and improvements in energy and well-being.

- Experiment with diverse recipes and meal plans to keep the diet enjoyable.

- Periodically reassess and adjust the approach to align with personal goals.

Dealing with Cravings and Emotional Eating: Strategies for Success

In this section, we address the challenges of cravings and emotional eating that individuals may encounter on their ketogenic journey. Understanding and managing these aspects are crucial for long-term success within the ketogenic lifestyle. Discover practical strategies to overcome cravings and emotional triggers, allowing you to maintain a healthy relationship with food.

1. Identify Triggers:

Understanding:

- Recognize situations, emotions, or stressors that trigger cravings and emotional eating.

Strategy:

- Keep a journal to track when cravings occur.

- Note the emotions or events associated with these cravings.

2. Mindful Eating:

Understanding:

- Mindful eating involves being present and aware of the eating experience.

Strategy:

- Slow down and savor each bite.

- Pay attention to flavors, textures, and satiety cues.

3. Choose Keto-Friendly Alternatives:

Understanding:

- Instead of succumbing to high-carb temptations, opt for satisfying keto-friendly alternatives.

Strategy:

- Keep keto snacks readily available.

- Choose snacks with healthy fats and proteins to curb cravings.

4. Emotional Support:

Understanding:

- Seek emotional support from friends, family, or a support group to navigate emotional eating.

Strategy:

- Share your challenges and goals with a trusted friend.

- Connect with online communities focused on ketogenic living.

5. Stress Management:

Understanding:

- Stress can contribute to emotional eating and cravings.

Strategy:

- Practice stress-reducing activities such as meditation, deep breathing, or yoga.

- Incorporate regular physical activity to manage stress levels.

6. Stay Hydrated:

Understanding:

- Dehydration can sometimes be mistaken for hunger or cravings.

Strategy:

- Drink an adequate amount of water throughout the day.

- Consider flavored water or herbal tea as a satisfying option.

7. Plan and Prepare Meals:

Understanding:

- Having nutritious, satisfying meals ready can prevent impulsive, high-carb choices.

Strategy:

- Plan meals in advance and prep ingredients.

- Batch-cook and store meals for convenience.

8. Practice Self-Compassion:

Understanding:

- Be kind to yourself and acknowledge that setbacks happen.

Strategy:

- Avoid self-criticism and guilt.

- Focus on making positive choices moving forward.

9. Distract Yourself:

Understanding:

- Distractions can help shift focus away from cravings.

Strategy:

- Engage in activities you enjoy or find relaxing.

- Take a short walk or immerse yourself in a hobby.

10. Optimize Nutrient Intake:

Understanding:

- Ensure that your ketogenic meals are well-balanced and meet nutritional needs.

Strategy:

- Include a variety of nutrient-dense foods in your diet.

- Consider consulting with a dietitian for personalized guidance.

Psychological Aspects of Cravings: Understanding and Overcoming

In this section, we delve into the psychological aspects of cravings, providing insights into the factors that contribute to the desire for certain foods. Understanding the psychological elements involved in cravings is essential for effectively managing and overcoming them within the context of a ketogenic lifestyle.

1. Emotional Triggers:

Understanding:

- Cravings are often linked to emotions, stress, boredom, or reward-seeking behavior.

Insight:

- Identifying emotional triggers can help address the root cause of cravings.

2. Reward System Activation:

Understanding:

- Certain foods trigger the brain's reward system, releasing feel-good neurotransmitters.

Insight:

- Cravings may be tied to the desire for pleasurable sensations associated with specific foods.

3. Habitual Patterns:

Understanding:

- Habits and routines can create associations between certain activities and specific foods.

Insight:

- Breaking habitual patterns can help reshape associations and reduce cravings.

4. Dopamine Release:

Understanding:

- Dopamine, a neurotransmitter, plays a role in pleasure and reward.

Insight:

- Cravings may be driven by the desire for a dopamine release associated with particular foods.

5. Sensory Appeal:

Understanding:

- The sensory appeal of certain foods, such as taste and texture, can contribute to cravings.

Insight:

- Identifying alternative keto-friendly foods with similar sensory qualities can be beneficial.

6. Social Influences:

Understanding:

- Social situations, peer influence, and cultural factors can impact food cravings.

Insight:

- Developing strategies to navigate social settings and make keto-friendly choices is crucial.

7. Cognitive Associations:

Understanding:

- Cognitive associations between comfort, pleasure, or stress relief and specific foods can drive cravings.

Insight:

- Shifting cognitive associations through mindful practices can help reshape cravings.

8. Coping Mechanisms:

Understanding:

- Cravings may serve as coping mechanisms for dealing with emotions or stress.

Insight:

- Exploring alternative coping strategies, such as exercise or relaxation techniques, can be beneficial.

9. Personalized Triggers:

Understanding:

- Cravings are unique to each individual, influenced by personal experiences and preferences.

Insight:

- Personalizing strategies for managing cravings is key to long-term success.

10. Cognitive Restructuring:

Understanding:

- Cognitive restructuring involves changing thought patterns and beliefs about food.

Insight:

- Shifting mindset from restriction to empowerment can positively impact cravings.

Mindful Eating Strategies: Cultivating Awareness for Ketogenic Success

In this section, we explore mindful eating strategies tailored to the ketogenic lifestyle. Mindful eating involves being present and attentive to the eating experience, fostering a healthier relationship with food. By incorporating these strategies, you can enhance your awareness, savor the flavors of keto-friendly meals, and make informed choices that align with your goals.

1. Slow Down and Savor:

Strategy:

- Take your time during meals and savor each bite.

- Put down utensils between bites to encourage a slower pace.

2. Engage Your Senses:

Strategy:

- Notice the colors, textures, and aromas of your food.

- Pay attention to how each bite feels in your mouth.

3. Portion Awareness:

Strategy:

- Use smaller plates and bowls to help with portion control.

- Listen to your body's signals of hunger and fullness.

4. Eliminate Distractions:

Strategy:

- Eat without distractions like TV or smartphones.

- Focus on the act of eating and the sensory experience.

5. Chew Thoroughly:

Strategy:

- Chew each bite thoroughly before swallowing.

- This aids in digestion and allows you to fully taste your food.

6. Tune into Hunger and Fullness:

Strategy:

- Check in with your hunger levels before and during meals.

- Stop eating when you feel satisfied, not overly full.

7. Recognize Emotional Hunger:

Strategy:

- Differentiate between physical hunger and emotional cravings.

- If not physically hungry, explore alternative ways to address emotions.

8. Practice Gratitude:

Strategy:

- Take a moment to appreciate the flavors, nutrients, and effort put into your meal.

- Cultivate a sense of gratitude for the nourishment your food provides.

9. Listen to Cravings Mindfully:

Strategy:

- When cravings arise, approach them with curiosity.

- Explore the sensations and emotions associated with cravings without judgment.

10. Be Present with Each Meal:

Strategy:

- Set aside time for meals without rushing.

- Focus on the experience of eating and the nourishment it provides.

11. Plan and Prepare Meals Mindfully:

Strategy:

- Engage in the process of meal planning and preparation.

- Connect with the ingredients and intentions behind each dish.

12. Practice Mindful Grocery Shopping:

Strategy:

- Make a shopping list and stick to it.

- Choose fresh, whole foods and avoid impulsive purchases.

Overcoming Plateaus: Strategies for Ketogenic Success

In this section, we address the common challenge of plateaus in the ketogenic journey. Plateaus occur when progress in weight loss or other health goals slows down or halts. Discover effective strategies to overcome plateaus and continue advancing toward your desired outcomes within the ketogenic lifestyle.

1. Reevaluate Macros and Caloric Intake:

Strategy:

- Review your current macronutrient ratios and overall caloric intake.

- Adjust the ratios or total calories based on your individual needs and goals.

2. Incorporate Intermittent Fasting:

Strategy:

- Introduce intermittent fasting by extending the time between meals.

- Experiment with different fasting windows to find what works for you.

3. Modify Exercise Routine:

Strategy:

- Evaluate your current exercise routine and consider making adjustments.

- Introduce new forms of exercise or increase intensity for variety.

4. Increase Physical Activity:

Strategy:

- Incorporate additional physical activity into your daily routine.

- Explore activities you enjoy, such as walking, cycling, or strength training.

5. Experiment with Carb Cycling:

Strategy:

- Try carb cycling by incorporating occasional higher-carb days.

- Monitor how your body responds and adjust accordingly.

6. Evaluate Stress Levels:

Strategy:

- Assess stress levels and explore stress-reducing activities.

- Incorporate practices such as meditation, yoga, or deep breathing.

7. Ensure Adequate Sleep:

Strategy:

- Prioritize sufficient and quality sleep.

- Create a bedtime routine to support a restful night's sleep.

8. Hydration and Electrolyte Balance:

Strategy:

- Ensure proper hydration and maintain electrolyte balance.

- Drink an adequate amount of water and consider electrolyte supplements if needed.

9. Focus on Whole Foods:

Strategy:

- Emphasize whole, nutrient-dense foods in your diet.

- Minimize processed foods and prioritize fresh, unprocessed options.

10. Track Non-Scale Victories:

Strategy:

- Shift focus from the scale to non-scale victories.

- Celebrate improvements in energy, mood, and overall well-being.

11. Assess Hormonal Health:

Strategy:

- Consider consulting with a healthcare professional to assess hormonal health.

- Address any potential imbalances that may be affecting progress.

12. Monitor Hidden Carbs:

Strategy:

- Review your food choices for hidden sources of carbohydrates.

- Check labels and ingredient lists to identify potential culprits.

13. Stay Consistent and Patient:

Strategy:

- Stay consistent with your ketogenic lifestyle.

- Be patient and recognize that plateaus are a normal part of the journey.

Identifying Plateaus and Stalls: Recognizing Signs of Slow Progress

In this section, we explore how to identify plateaus and stalls in your ketogenic journey. Recognizing the signs of slow progress is crucial for implementing targeted strategies to overcome challenges and continue advancing toward your health and wellness goals within the ketogenic lifestyle.

1. Monitoring Weight Loss Trends:

Signs:

- Lack of significant weight loss over an extended period.

- Fluctuations within a small weight range without a downward trend.

Action:

- Track your weight consistently and observe patterns.

- Look for prolonged periods of minimal change.

2. Energy and Performance Plateau:

Signs:

- Stalled improvements in energy levels and overall performance.

- Lack of noticeable advancements in exercise or physical activities.

Action:

- Evaluate changes in energy levels and exercise performance.

- Consider adjusting your workout routine or intensity.

3. No Change in Body Measurements:

Signs:

- Measurements of waist, hips, and other areas show little to no change.

- Clothing sizes remain the same despite adherence to the ketogenic diet.

Action:

- Regularly measure key areas to track changes.
- Assess whether clothing feels looser or tighter.

4. Constant Hunger or Cravings:

Signs:

- Persistent feelings of hunger or cravings.
- Difficulty adhering to the ketogenic diet due to increased appetite.

Action:

- Review your current macronutrient ratios.
- Ensure you are consuming enough healthy fats for satiety.

5. Plateau in Physical Fitness:

Signs:

- Stalled progress in strength, endurance, or other fitness goals.
- Lack of improvements in physical capabilities despite consistent efforts.

Action:

- Assess your workout routine and intensity.
- Consider incorporating new exercises or increasing resistance.

6. Lack of Non-Scale Victories:

Signs:

- Limited improvements in non-scale victories, such as mood or mental clarity.
- Few noticeable positive changes beyond weight loss.

Action:

- Shift focus to non-scale victories for a holistic view of progress.
- Celebrate improvements in overall well-being.

7. Emotional or Mental Stalls:

Signs:

- Plateau in mental clarity or improvements in mood.

- Persistent challenges in managing stress or emotional well-being.

Action:

- Evaluate lifestyle factors affecting mental health.

- Introduce stress-reducing practices and mindfulness.

8. Digestive Issues and Inflammation:

Signs:

- Persistent digestive discomfort or inflammation.

- Lack of improvement in gut health markers.

Action:

- Assess dietary choices and potential triggers.

- Consider incorporating gut-friendly foods and supplements.

9. Consistency in Food Choices:

Signs:

- Limited variety in food choices and meals.

- Lack of experimentation with new keto-friendly recipes.

Action:

- Explore diverse recipes and ingredients.

- Introduce variety to enhance nutrient intake.

10. Emotional Awareness:

Signs:

- Emotional eating habits persist despite efforts.

- Challenges in addressing the psychological aspects of cravings.

Action:

- Cultivate emotional awareness through mindfulness.

- Seek support for managing emotional triggers.

Adjusting Diet and Exercise for Progress: Tailoring Your Approach within Ketogenic Living

In this section, we explore strategies for adjusting your diet and exercise to overcome plateaus and promote continued progress within the ketogenic lifestyle. By tailoring your approach, you can optimize your nutrition and physical activity to align with your evolving goals and address specific challenges you may encounter on your journey.

1. Reassessing Macronutrient Ratios:

Strategy:

- Review your current macronutrient ratios (fat, protein, carbs).

- Adjust ratios based on individual needs, activity levels, and goals.

2. Implementing Carb Cycling:

Strategy:

- Experiment with carb cycling by incorporating occasional higher-carb days.

- Observe how your body responds and adjust the frequency as needed.

3. Introducing Periodic Fasting:

Strategy:

- Implement intermittent fasting by extending the time between meals.

- Explore different fasting windows to support your metabolic flexibility.

4. Varying Caloric Intake:

Strategy:

- Consider cycling caloric intake to prevent metabolic adaptation.

- Alternate between periods of slightly higher and lower caloric intake.

5. Exploring New Keto-Friendly Foods:

Strategy:

- Introduce a variety of keto-friendly foods and ingredients.

- Explore new recipes to enhance nutrient diversity.

6. Modifying Exercise Routine:

Strategy:

- Evaluate your current exercise routine, including type, duration, and intensity.

- Introduce new exercises or increase intensity to challenge your body.

7. Incorporating High-Intensity Interval Training (HIIT):

Strategy:

- Integrate HIIT workouts to boost metabolic rate and fat burning.

- Include short bursts of intense exercise followed by periods of rest.

8. Increasing Physical Activity:

Strategy:

- Explore additional ways to increase daily physical activity.

- Incorporate activities you enjoy, such as hiking, biking, or dancing.

9. Periodic Refeeds:

Strategy:

- Consider periodic refeeds with slightly higher carb intake.

- Monitor how refeeds impact your energy levels and overall well-being.

10. Prioritizing Sleep and Recovery:

Strategy:

- Ensure sufficient and quality sleep for optimal recovery.

- Incorporate relaxation practices to support overall well-being.

11. Stress Management Techniques:

Strategy:

- Implement stress-reducing techniques, such as meditation or deep breathing.

- Prioritize activities that promote mental and emotional well-being.

12. Experimenting with Fasting Windows:

Strategy:

- Experiment with different fasting windows to find what suits you.

- Adjust the duration and frequency based on your body's response.

13. Monitoring and Adjusting:

Strategy:

- Regularly monitor progress and adjust your approach as needed.

- Stay attuned to your body's signals and make informed decisions.

Addressing Common Concerns for Women: Navigating Unique Aspects of Ketogenic Living

In this section, we address common concerns specific to women within the context of ketogenic living. Understanding and addressing these unique aspects can contribute to a more personalized and supportive approach, enhancing the overall experience for women pursuing the ketogenic lifestyle.

1. Menstrual Cycle and Hormonal Fluctuations:

Concern:

- Women may experience changes in menstrual cycles or hormonal fluctuations.

Address:

- Monitor menstrual cycles and note any irregularities.

- Prioritize nutrient-dense foods to support hormonal balance.

- Consult with a healthcare professional if concerns persist.

2. Pregnancy and Ketogenic Diet:

Concern:

- Women who are pregnant or planning to conceive may have concerns about the ketogenic diet.

Address:

- Consult with a healthcare provider before starting or continuing a ketogenic diet during pregnancy.

- Ensure nutrient adequacy through a well-balanced ketogenic approach.

3. Adjusting Macronutrient Ratios:

Concern:

- Women may need different macronutrient ratios than men due to metabolic and hormonal differences.

Address:

- Individualize macronutrient ratios based on energy needs, activity levels, and health goals.

- Monitor how the chosen ratios impact energy, performance, and overall well-being.

4. Protein Intake for Muscle Health:

Concern:

- Adequate protein intake is essential for muscle health, and women may have specific protein needs.

Address:

- Determine protein needs based on individual factors such as activity level, muscle mass, and goals.

- Include a variety of protein sources to ensure essential amino acid intake.

5. Fat Consumption and Energy Levels:

Concern:

- Balancing fat consumption for energy needs and weight management.

Address:

- Adjust fat intake based on energy requirements and weight management goals.

- Prioritize healthy fats such as avocados, olive oil, and nuts.

6. Special Considerations for Hormonal Health:

Concern:

- Hormonal health can be influenced by dietary choices and lifestyle factors.

Address:

- Focus on nutrient-dense foods to support hormonal balance.

- Consider consulting with a healthcare professional for personalized advice.

7. Impact on Thyroid Function:

Concern:

- Ketogenic diets may influence thyroid function.

Address:

- Monitor thyroid function through regular testing.

- Consult with a healthcare provider to ensure thyroid health is addressed appropriately.

8. Managing Menopausal Symptoms:

Concern:

- Women experiencing menopausal symptoms may seek strategies within the ketogenic lifestyle.

Address:

- Prioritize nutrient-dense foods to support overall health during menopause.

- Consider lifestyle factors and consult with a healthcare professional for tailored guidance.

Hair Loss, Skin Changes, and Other Side Effects: Understanding and Managing Potential Challenges

In this section, we address potential side effects that individuals may encounter while following a ketogenic lifestyle. Understanding these effects and implementing strategies to manage them can contribute to a more informed and balanced experience within the ketogenic journey.

1. Hair Loss:

Understanding:

- Some individuals may experience hair loss during the initial stages of a ketogenic diet.

Management:

- Ensure sufficient protein intake to support hair health.

- Consider incorporating nutrient-dense foods and supplements if needed.

- Be patient, as hair loss may be temporary and related to dietary changes.

2. Skin Changes:

Understanding:

- Skin changes, including dryness or acne, may occur due to shifts in dietary patterns.

Management:

- Stay hydrated to support skin hydration.

- Include sources of healthy fats to promote skin health.

- Monitor skin changes and consult with a dermatologist if needed.

3. Electrolyte Imbalance:

Understanding:

- Changes in electrolyte balance can occur, leading to symptoms like fatigue, muscle cramps, or headaches.

Management:

- Ensure an adequate intake of electrolytes (sodium, potassium, magnesium).

- Include electrolyte-rich foods in the diet.

- Consider electrolyte supplements if needed, especially during the adaptation phase.

4. Digestive Issues:

Understanding:

- Some individuals may experience digestive issues such as constipation or diarrhea.

Management:

- Ensure sufficient fiber intake through vegetables and low-carb sources.

- Stay hydrated and consider adding sources of healthy fats, such as avocados and olive oil.

- Experiment with different fiber sources to find what works best for you.

5. Increased Cholesterol Levels:

Understanding:

- Changes in cholesterol levels may occur in response to a high-fat diet.

Management:

- Monitor cholesterol levels regularly.

- Focus on overall cardiovascular health by including heart-healthy fats and staying active.

- Consult with a healthcare professional for personalized guidance.

6. Keto Flu:

Understanding:

- Some individuals may experience symptoms known as the "keto flu" during the initial adaptation phase.

Management:

- Stay hydrated and ensure adequate electrolyte intake.

- Gradually transition into the ketogenic diet to allow the body to adapt.

- Be patient, as symptoms usually subside within a few days.

7. Insomnia or Sleep Changes:

Understanding:

- Sleep patterns may be affected during the initial stages of a ketogenic diet.

Management:

- Establish a consistent sleep routine.

- Limit caffeine intake, especially in the evening.

- Incorporate relaxation techniques to promote restful sleep.

8. Mental and Emotional Changes:

Understanding:

- Some individuals may experience mental or emotional changes, including mood swings or irritability.

Management:

- Ensure sufficient intake of micronutrients and prioritize nutrient-dense foods.

- Practice stress-reducing activities such as meditation or deep breathing.

- Seek support from friends, family, or a healthcare professional if needed.

Seeking Professional Guidance:

While this textbook provides valuable information on ketogenic living for women, it is essential to recognize that every individual's health needs are unique. Therefore, before making significant dietary changes or embarking on a new lifestyle, it is highly recommended to seek professional guidance from qualified healthcare professionals.

Consulting with a registered dietitian, nutritionist, or healthcare provider can help assess your current health status, identify any specific dietary requirements or restrictions, and tailor recommendations to meet your individual needs. They can provide personalized advice, monitor your progress, and address any concerns or questions you may have along the way.

Additionally, if you have pre-existing medical conditions, are pregnant or breastfeeding, or are taking medications, it is especially important to consult with your healthcare provider before making any dietary changes. They can offer guidance on how to safely incorporate ketogenic principles into your lifestyle while ensuring optimal health and well-being.

Remember, your health is invaluable, and professional guidance can provide you with the support and expertise needed to make informed decisions about your dietary choices and overall wellness journey.

Exercise and Ketogenic Living: Integrating Physical Activity for Optimal

Health

In this section, we explore the integration of exercise within the context of ketogenic living. Physical activity plays a crucial role in supporting overall health, optimizing ketosis, and enhancing the benefits of a ketogenic lifestyle. Discover practical insights and strategies to align your exercise routine with your ketogenic goals.

1. Types of Exercise:

Insight:

- Different types of exercise offer unique benefits.

- Include a combination of aerobic, strength training, and flexibility exercises.

2. Aerobic Exercise:

Insight:

- Aerobic exercise, such as walking, jogging, or cycling, supports cardiovascular health.

- Engage in activities that elevate your heart rate and promote endurance.

3. Strength Training:

Insight:

- Strength training builds muscle mass and supports metabolic health.

- Include resistance training with weights or bodyweight exercises.

4. High-Intensity Interval Training (HIIT):

Insight:

- HIIT involves short bursts of intense activity followed by rest.

- Enhances fat burning and metabolic flexibility.

5. Flexibility and Mobility Exercises:

Insight:

- Incorporate stretching and mobility exercises to improve flexibility.

- Enhances joint health and reduces the risk of injuries.

6. Timing of Exercise:

Insight:

- Consider the timing of your workouts based on personal preferences and energy levels.

- Some individuals prefer morning workouts for increased energy throughout the day.

7. Exercise Adaptation during Transition:

Insight:

- During the initial stages of transitioning to a ketogenic diet, energy levels may fluctuate.

- Adjust exercise intensity and duration accordingly.

8. Listen to Your Body:

Insight:

- Pay attention to your body's signals during and after exercise.

- Modify your routine based on how you feel, especially during the adaptation phase.

9. Hydration and Electrolyte Balance:

Insight:

- Stay hydrated before, during, and after exercise.

- Ensure proper electrolyte balance to prevent fatigue and muscle cramps.

10. Post-Exercise Nutrition:

Insight:

- Consider post-exercise nutrition to support recovery.

- Include a combination of protein and healthy fats in post-workout meals.

11. Experiment with Carb Timing:

Insight:

- Some individuals may benefit from strategic carb intake around workouts.

- Experiment with carb timing based on personal response and goals.

12. Monitor Energy Levels:

Insight:

- Pay attention to how your energy levels and performance are influenced by the ketogenic diet.

- Adjust macronutrient ratios if needed for optimal performance.

13. Incorporate Enjoyable Activities:

Insight:

- Choose activities you enjoy to make exercise a sustainable part of your routine.

- Explore outdoor activities, group classes, or sports.

14. Consistency is Key:

Insight:

- Consistency in your exercise routine is essential for long-term benefits.

- Find a schedule and types of exercise that fit into your lifestyle.

Incorporating Exercise into Ketogenic Lifestyle: A Practical Guide

In this section, we provide a practical guide for seamlessly integrating exercise into your ketogenic lifestyle. Whether you're a beginner or experienced in fitness, these strategies will help you optimize the synergy between exercise and ketosis, fostering overall health and well-being.

1. Start with Realistic Goals:

Strategy:

- Set achievable and realistic exercise goals.

- Consider factors such as fitness level, time availability, and preferences.

2. Choose Enjoyable Activities:

Strategy:

- Select exercises and activities you genuinely enjoy.

- This increases the likelihood of adherence to your workout routine.

3. Create a Consistent Schedule:

Strategy:

- Establish a regular exercise schedule that aligns with your daily routine.

- Consistency is key to building a sustainable habit.

4. Mix Aerobic and Strength Training:

Strategy:

- Include a combination of aerobic (e.g., walking, jogging) and strength training exercises.

- This promotes cardiovascular health and muscle strength.

5. Gradual Progression:

Strategy:

- Start with manageable intensity and duration, especially if you're new to exercise.

- Gradually increase intensity and duration over time.

6. Listen to Your Body:

Strategy:

- Pay attention to how your body responds to exercise.

- Modify your routine based on energy levels and recovery.

7. Adapt to Your Ketogenic Journey:

Strategy:

- During the initial stages of a ketogenic diet, energy levels may fluctuate.

- Adjust exercise intensity and duration accordingly.

8. Hydrate and Balance Electrolytes:

Strategy:

- Stay well-hydrated before, during, and after exercise.

- Ensure proper electrolyte balance to prevent fatigue and cramps.

9. Post-Workout Nutrition:

Strategy:

- Consider post-workout nutrition with a focus on protein and healthy fats.

- Support recovery and muscle repair with a well-balanced meal.

10. Experiment with Carb Timing:

Strategy:

- Some individuals may benefit from strategic carb intake around workouts.

- Experiment with carb timing based on personal response and goals.

11. Include Flexibility and Mobility:

Strategy:

- Incorporate stretching and mobility exercises into your routine.

- Improve flexibility and reduce the risk of injuries.

12. Outdoor Activities:

Strategy:

- Explore outdoor activities for a change of scenery.

- Hiking, biking, or nature walks can be enjoyable forms of exercise.

13. Involve Social Support:

Strategy:

- Exercise with friends or join group classes for social support.

- Make fitness a social and enjoyable experience.

14. Monitor Progress:

Strategy:

- Track your exercise progress and celebrate achievements.

- Adjust your goals as you advance in your fitness journey.

Benefits of Physical Activity on Ketosis: Maximizing the Synergy

In this section, we explore the powerful synergy between physical activity and ketosis. Understanding the benefits of exercise on ketosis can inspire and motivate individuals to incorporate regular physical activity into their ketogenic lifestyle.

1. Enhanced Fat Burning:

Insight:

- Exercise, especially aerobic activities, increases fat oxidation.

- Promotes the utilization of fatty acids for energy, aligning with ketosis.

2. Improved Metabolic Flexibility:

Insight:

- Regular exercise enhances the body's ability to switch between different energy sources.

- Supports metabolic flexibility, a key aspect of ketogenic adaptation.

3. Accelerated Ketone Production:

Insight:

- Exercise can stimulate the production of ketones.

- Enhances the transition into ketosis and sustains ketone levels.

4. Increased Insulin Sensitivity:

Insight:

- Physical activity improves insulin sensitivity.

- Supports better blood sugar control and aids in maintaining ketosis.

5. Muscle Preservation and Growth:

Insight:

- Resistance training helps preserve and build lean muscle mass.

- Muscle tissue contributes to overall metabolic health and ketosis.

6. Appetite Regulation:

Insight:

- Exercise can regulate appetite hormones.

- Supports better control over food intake, aiding in adherence to a ketogenic diet.

7. Enhanced Weight Management:

Insight:

- Regular physical activity contributes to weight loss and weight maintenance.

- Complements the ketogenic diet for effective weight management.

8. Stress Reduction:

Insight:

- Exercise is a natural stress reliever.

- Reduces cortisol levels, supporting overall hormonal balance and ketosis.

9. Improved Sleep Quality:

Insight:

- Regular physical activity promotes better sleep quality.

- Supports overall well-being and enhances the benefits of ketosis.

10. Mood and Cognitive Benefits:

Insight:

- Exercise has positive effects on mood and cognitive function.

- Supports mental well-being, contributing to a holistic ketogenic lifestyle.

11. Optimal Mitochondrial Function:

Insight:

- Physical activity promotes mitochondrial health.

- Enhances the efficiency of energy production, a key aspect of ketosis.

12. Sustainable Ketogenic Adherence:

Insight:

- Incorporating exercise makes the ketogenic lifestyle more sustainable.

- Creates a positive feedback loop, reinforcing the benefits of both ketosis and physical activity.

13. Cardiovascular Health Support:

Insight:

- Aerobic exercise contributes to cardiovascular health.

- Aligns with the overall health goals of individuals following a ketogenic lifestyle.

14. Long-Term Health Benefits:

Insight:

- Regular physical activity is associated with long-term health benefits.

- Enhances the positive impact of the ketogenic lifestyle on overall health.

Finding the Right Exercise Routine: Tailoring Physical Activity to Your Ketogenic Journey

In this section, we delve into the process of finding the right exercise routine that aligns with your ketogenic journey. Understanding your preferences, fitness level, and goals is key to creating a sustainable and enjoyable exercise plan within the context of a ketogenic lifestyle.

1. Assess Your Fitness Level:

Strategy:

- Begin by assessing your current fitness level.

- Consider factors such as cardiovascular endurance, strength, and flexibility.

2. Define Your Goals:

Strategy:

- Clearly define your exercise goals within the context of your ketogenic journey.

- Whether it's weight loss, muscle gain, or overall well-being, having specific goals guides your routine.

3. Identify Preferred Activities:

Strategy:

- List activities you enjoy or are curious to try.

- Choose exercises that align with your preferences for a more sustainable routine.

4. Consider Time Availability:

Strategy:

- Evaluate how much time you can dedicate to exercise each day or week.

- Opt for routines that fit seamlessly into your schedule.

5. Mix Aerobic and Strength Training:

Strategy:

- Aim for a balanced combination of aerobic (cardio) and strength training exercises.

- This provides overall fitness benefits and complements the ketogenic lifestyle.

6. Explore Different Exercise Modalities:

Strategy:

- Experiment with various exercise modalities.

- This could include activities like walking, running, cycling, weightlifting, yoga, or group classes.

7. Adapt to Your Preferences:

Strategy:

- Tailor your routine to your preferences and personality.

- If you enjoy social activities, consider group classes or team sports. If you prefer solitude, activities like hiking or solo workouts may be ideal.

8. Gradual Progression:

Strategy:

- Start with a routine that matches your current fitness level.

- Gradually increase intensity and duration to avoid burnout or injury.

9. Include Flexibility and Mobility:

Strategy:

- Incorporate stretching and mobility exercises to improve flexibility.

- This contributes to overall joint health and reduces the risk of injuries.

10. Listen to Your Body:

Strategy:

- Pay attention to how your body responds to different exercises.

- Adjust your routine based on energy levels, recovery, and any discomfort.

11. Mix Indoor and Outdoor Activities:

Strategy:

- Include a mix of indoor and outdoor activities.

- Outdoor activities provide a change of scenery and connection with nature.

12. Consistency Over Intensity:

Strategy:

- Prioritize consistency in your exercise routine.

- Sustainable, regular activity is more beneficial than sporadic intense workouts.

13. Seek Professional Guidance:

Strategy:

- Consider consulting with fitness professionals or trainers.

- They can provide personalized guidance based on your goals and fitness level.

14. Enjoy the Process:

Strategy:

- Find joy in your exercise routine.

- Whether it's the satisfaction of completing a workout or the enjoyment of the activity itself, a positive mindset enhances adherence.

- Whether it's the satisfaction of completing a workout or the enjoyment of the activity itself, a positive mindset enhances adherence.

Optimizing Workouts for Women on a Ketogenic Diet: Personalized Strategies for Success

In this section, we explore personalized strategies to optimize workouts specifically for women on a ketogenic diet. Understanding the unique needs and considerations of women allows for a tailored approach to physical activity within the context of ketosis.

1. Hormonal Considerations:

Strategy:

- Be aware of hormonal fluctuations throughout the menstrual cycle.

- Adapt workout intensity and type based on energy levels during different phases.

2. Adjusting Macronutrient Intake:

Strategy:

- Consider adjusting macronutrient ratios around workouts.

- Ensure sufficient protein intake for muscle support and recovery.

3. Tailoring Strength Training:

Strategy:

- Incorporate strength training exercises to support muscle preservation and growth.

- Adjust resistance and volume based on individual fitness levels.

4. Cardiovascular Exercise:

Strategy:

- Include cardiovascular exercises for overall heart health.

- Adjust intensity and duration based on personal preferences and fitness goals.

5. Prioritize Flexibility and Mobility:

Strategy:

- Emphasize flexibility and mobility exercises to support joint health.

- Include activities such as yoga or dynamic stretching.

6. Post-Workout Nutrition:

Strategy:

- Consider post-workout nutrition with a focus on protein and healthy fats.

- Support muscle recovery and replenish energy stores.

7. Carb Timing and Cycling:

Strategy:

- Experiment with strategic carb intake around workouts.

- Evaluate how this influences energy levels and workout performance.

8. Mind-Body Connection:

Strategy:

- Cultivate a mind-body connection during workouts.

- Practice mindfulness to enhance the overall exercise experience.

9. Adaptation During Transition:

Strategy:

- Be mindful of energy fluctuations during the transition to a ketogenic diet.

- Adjust workout intensity based on energy levels.

10. Consideration for Menopausal Women:

Strategy:

- Recognize the impact of menopause on energy levels and recovery.

- Adapt workout routines to accommodate individual needs during this phase.

11. Social Support and Accountability:

Strategy:

- Seek social support for motivation and accountability.

- Join group classes or find a workout buddy to enhance enjoyment and adherence.

12. Listen to Your Body:

Strategy:

- Pay close attention to your body's signals.

- Adjust workouts based on how you feel, allowing for flexibility in your routine.

13. Adjusting Intensity During Pregnancy:

Strategy:

- If pregnant, consult with healthcare professionals before continuing or starting a workout routine.

- Modify workout intensity and type based on trimester and individual circumstances.

14. Celebrate Non-Scale Victories:

Strategy:

- Acknowledge and celebrate non-scale victories related to fitness and well-being.

- Shift the focus beyond weight-related goals.

Strength Training and Muscle Preservation: Building Resilience on a Ketogenic Journey

In this section, we delve into the significance of strength training for women on a ketogenic diet. Understanding how strength training contributes to muscle preservation and overall well-being empowers individuals to incorporate this essential component into their ketogenic lifestyle.

1. Importance of Strength Training:

Insight:

- Strength training is crucial for preserving and building lean muscle mass.

- Contributes to metabolic health, body composition, and overall strength.

2. Muscle Preservation on a Ketogenic Diet:

Insight:

- While on a ketogenic diet, strength training becomes a key factor in preserving existing muscle mass.

- Helps prevent muscle loss during weight loss or dietary changes.

3. Adaptations in Resistance Training:

Insight:

- Adapt resistance training based on individual fitness levels.

- Gradually increase resistance to challenge muscles and promote adaptation.

4. Full-Body Workouts:

Insight:

- Incorporate full-body strength training workouts.

- Targets multiple muscle groups, optimizing efficiency and effectiveness.

5. Compound Exercises:

Insight:

- Include compound exercises that engage multiple joints and muscle groups.

- Examples include squats, deadlifts, and bench press.

6. Progressive Overload:

Insight:

- Implement progressive overload to stimulate muscle growth.

- Gradually increase the resistance, volume, or intensity of workouts.

7. Resistance Bands and Bodyweight Exercises:

Insight:

- Utilize resistance bands and bodyweight exercises.

- Ideal for home workouts or when access to traditional gym equipment is limited.

8. Focus on Form and Technique:

Insight:

- Prioritize proper form and technique during strength training.

- Reduces the risk of injuries and maximizes effectiveness.

9. Individualization of Workouts:

Insight:

- Tailor strength training workouts to individual preferences and goals.

- Consider factors such as workout frequency, duration, and specific muscle groups.

10. Integration with Cardiovascular Exercise:

Insight:

- Integrate strength training with cardiovascular exercise for a well-rounded fitness routine.

- Enhances overall cardiovascular health and supports ketosis.

11. Recovery and Rest Days:

Insight:

- Allow for adequate recovery between strength training sessions.

- Incorporate rest days to prevent overtraining and support muscle recovery.

12. Hormonal Benefits:

Insight:

- Strength training has positive effects on hormonal balance.

- Supports the production of growth hormone and contributes to overall well-being.

13. Adapting During Transition:

Insight:

- During the transition to a ketogenic diet, adapt strength training intensity based on energy levels.

- Gradually increase intensity as the body becomes accustomed to ketosis.

14. Consistency in Routine:

Insight:

- Prioritize consistency in strength training.

- Regular sessions contribute to long-term muscle preservation and overall fitness.

Cardiovascular Exercise and Endurance: Elevating Ketogenic Fitness

In this section, we explore the role of cardiovascular exercise in enhancing endurance and overall fitness within the context of a ketogenic lifestyle. Understanding the benefits and strategies for incorporating cardio can empower individuals to optimize their fitness journey.

1. Cardiovascular Exercise and Ketosis:

Insight:

- Cardiovascular exercise complements the ketogenic lifestyle by promoting endurance and cardiovascular health.

- Enhances the body's ability to efficiently utilize fat for energy.

2. Types of Cardiovascular Exercise:

Insight:

- Include a variety of cardiovascular exercises.

- Options include walking, running, cycling, swimming, and high-intensity interval training (HIIT).

3. Benefits of Cardio for Endurance:

Insight:

- Regular cardio improves aerobic capacity and endurance.

- Supports sustained physical activity and enhances overall fitness.

4. Adaptation to Fat as a Fuel Source:

Insight:

- Cardiovascular exercise encourages the body to adapt to using fat as a primary fuel source.

- Aligns with the metabolic shift induced by the ketogenic diet.

5. Intensity and Duration:

Insight:

- Adjust the intensity and duration of cardio based on fitness level and goals.

- Incorporate both moderate-intensity and high-intensity sessions for optimal benefits.

6. Interval Training for Efficiency:

Insight:

- High-Intensity Interval Training (HIIT) is an efficient form of cardio.

- Alternating between short bursts of intense effort and rest enhances cardiovascular fitness.

7. Low-Impact Options:

Insight:

- Consider low-impact cardio options, especially for individuals with joint concerns.

- Activities like swimming or cycling can provide effective cardiovascular exercise with reduced impact.

8. Consistency is Key:

Insight:

- Prioritize consistency in cardiovascular exercise.

- Regular sessions contribute to improved endurance and overall health.

9. Integration with Strength Training:

Insight:

- Integrate cardiovascular exercise with strength training for a well-rounded fitness routine.

- Enhances both cardiovascular and muscular fitness.

10. Listen to Your Body:

Insight:

- Pay attention to how your body responds to cardio.

- Adjust intensity and duration based on energy levels and recovery.

11. Individualized Approach:

Insight:

- Tailor cardio workouts to individual preferences and goals.

- Experiment with different activities to find what you enjoy most.

12. Monitor Progress:

Insight:

- Track progress in cardiovascular fitness.

- Use metrics such as time, distance, or perceived exertion to monitor improvements.

13. Post-Cardio Nutrition:

Insight:

- Consider post-cardio nutrition with a focus on replenishing energy stores.

- Optimize recovery with a well-balanced meal or snack.

14. Enjoyable Cardio Activities:

Insight:

- Choose cardiovascular activities that you find enjoyable.

- This increases the likelihood of adherence to your fitness routine.

Supplements and Support: Enhancing Your Ketogenic Journey

In this section, we explore the role of supplements and additional support to optimize the ketogenic journey for women. Understanding the potential benefits of specific supplements and seeking additional support can contribute to a well-rounded and personalized approach to ketosis.

1. Essential Supplements for Ketogenic Living:

Insight:

- Consider essential supplements to support nutritional needs on a ketogenic diet.

- Common supplements include electrolytes (sodium, potassium, magnesium), omega-3 fatty acids, and vitamin D.

2. Electrolyte Balance:

Insight:

- Maintain electrolyte balance, especially during the adaptation phase.

- Electrolyte supplements or electrolyte-rich foods can help prevent imbalances.

3. Omega-3 Fatty Acids:

Insight:

- Include omega-3 fatty acids for heart health and inflammation support.

- Sources include fish oil, flaxseeds, chia seeds, and walnuts.

4. Vitamin D Supplementation:

Insight:

- Consider vitamin D supplementation, especially if sunlight exposure is limited.

- Supports bone health and overall well-being.

5. Multivitamin and Mineral Supplements:

Insight:

- A high-quality multivitamin can provide additional micronutrient support.

- Ensures a broad spectrum of essential vitamins and minerals.

6. Individualized Nutrient Needs:

Insight:

- Assess individual nutrient needs based on factors such as age, health status, and dietary preferences.

- Personalize supplement intake accordingly.

7. Consultation with Healthcare Professionals:

Insight:

- Consult with healthcare professionals before starting any supplements.

- Ensure compatibility with individual health conditions and medications.

8. Support from Registered Dietitians:

Insight:

- Seek guidance from registered dietitians specializing in ketogenic nutrition.

- Receive personalized advice and support for optimal dietary choices.

9. Peer Support Groups:

Insight:

- Join peer support groups or communities focused on ketogenic living.

- Share experiences, tips, and encouragement with like-minded individuals.

10. Mind-Body Support:

Insight:

- Incorporate mind-body practices for holistic well-being.

- Activities such as meditation, yoga, or mindfulness can complement the ketogenic lifestyle.

11. Regular Health Checkups:

Insight:

- Schedule regular health checkups to monitor overall well-being.

- Address any concerns or adjustments needed in consultation with healthcare professionals.

12. Genetic Testing for Personalized Nutrition:

Insight:

- Consider genetic testing for personalized nutrition insights.

- Understand how genetic factors may influence nutrient metabolism and dietary response.

13. Hormonal Health Support:

Insight:

- Explore hormonal health support options if needed.

- Consult with healthcare professionals or specialists in women's health.

14. Periodic Nutritional Assessments:

Insight:

- Periodically assess nutritional needs and adjust dietary and supplement strategies accordingly.

- Adapt to changes in health status, lifestyle, or fitness goals.

Essential Nutritional Supplements: Nourishing Your Ketogenic Path

In this section, we delve into the essential nutritional supplements that can support and enhance the ketogenic journey for women. Understanding the specific needs of a ketogenic lifestyle allows for targeted supplementation to optimize overall health and well-being.

1. Electrolyte Supplements:

Insight:

- Maintain electrolyte balance with supplements containing sodium, potassium, and magnesium.

- Especially important during the initial stages of ketosis.

2. Omega-3 Fatty Acids:

Insight:

- Include omega-3 fatty acids to support heart health and reduce inflammation.

- Sources include fish oil, krill oil, flaxseeds, chia seeds, and walnuts.

3. Vitamin D:

Insight:

- Consider vitamin D supplementation, especially if sunlight exposure is limited.

- Essential for bone health and overall well-being.

4. Multivitamin and Mineral Supplements:

Insight:

- Opt for a high-quality multivitamin to fill potential nutrient gaps.

- Ensures a broad spectrum of essential vitamins and minerals.

5. B Vitamins:

Insight:

- Supplement with B vitamins, including B12 and folate.

- Important for energy metabolism and neurological health.

6. Vitamin K2:

Insight:

- Include vitamin K2 for bone health and optimal calcium metabolism.

- Found in fermented foods and supplements.

7. Fiber Supplements:

Insight:

- If needed, incorporate fiber supplements to support digestive health.

- Choose options like psyllium husk or glucomannan.

8. Collagen Supplements:

Insight:

- Consider collagen supplements for joint health, skin elasticity, and connective tissue support.

- Enhances overall structural integrity.

9. Magnesium:

Insight:

- Supplement with magnesium to support muscle function, relaxation, and sleep.

- Various forms are available, such as magnesium citrate or magnesium glycinate.

10. Calcium:

Insight:

- Ensure adequate calcium intake, either through dietary sources or supplements.

- Important for bone health and overall mineral balance.

11. Iron:

Insight:

- Monitor iron levels and supplement if necessary, especially for women with increased needs.

- Supportive of energy metabolism and oxygen transport.

12. Potassium:

Insight:

- Consider potassium supplementation, particularly if dietary intake is insufficient.

- Supports muscle function and electrolyte balance.

13. Zinc:

Insight:

- Supplement with zinc for immune function and skin health.

- Found in various foods and available as a supplement.

14. Coenzyme Q10 (CoQ10):

Insight:

- Consider CoQ10 supplementation for antioxidant support and energy production.

- Especially relevant for those on a ketogenic diet.

Before incorporating any supplements, it's crucial to consult with healthcare professionals to ensure compatibility with individual health conditions and medications. Understanding your unique nutritional needs allows for targeted and effective supplementation on your ketogenic journey.

Vitamins and Minerals for Ketogenic Dieters: A Comprehensive Guide

In this section, we explore the specific vitamins and minerals that play a crucial role in supporting the health and well-being of individuals following a ketogenic diet. Understanding these essential nutrients allows for targeted dietary choices to optimize nutritional intake on the ketogenic journey.

1. Vitamin D:

Insight:

- Vital for bone health and overall well-being.

- Sources include fatty fish, egg yolks, and supplementation if sunlight exposure is limited.

2. Vitamin K2:

Insight:

- Supports bone health and optimal calcium metabolism.

- Found in fermented foods, organ meats, and certain cheeses.

3. B Vitamins:

Insight:

- Essential for energy metabolism and neurological health.

- Sources include meat, fish, eggs, leafy greens, and supplementation if needed.

4. Vitamin C:

Insight:

- Important for immune function and collagen synthesis.
- Obtain from low-carb vegetables like bell peppers and broccoli.

5. Vitamin A:

Insight:

- Supports vision, immune function, and skin health.
- Found in liver, eggs, and leafy greens.

6. Vitamin E:

Insight:

- Acts as an antioxidant, protecting cells from damage.
- Sources include nuts, seeds, and certain oils.

7. Calcium:

Insight:

- Crucial for bone health and overall mineral balance.
- Obtain from dairy products, leafy greens, or supplementation if necessary.

8. Magnesium:

Insight:

- Supports muscle function, relaxation, and sleep.
- Sources include nuts, seeds, leafy greens, and supplementation if needed.

9. Potassium:

Insight:

- Important for muscle function and electrolyte balance.
- Found in avocados, leafy greens, and supplementation if dietary intake is insufficient.

10. Sodium:

Insight:

- Maintains electrolyte balance, especially during ketosis.

- Consume from natural sources like salt or electrolyte supplements.

11. Phosphorus:

Insight:

- Essential for bone health and energy metabolism.

- Found in meat, dairy, nuts, and seeds.

12. Iron:

Insight:

- Supports oxygen transport and energy metabolism.

- Sources include meat, poultry, fish, and leafy greens.

13. Zinc:

Insight:

- Important for immune function and skin health.

- Found in meat, dairy, nuts, and seeds.

14. Selenium:

Insight:

- Acts as an antioxidant and supports thyroid function.

- Sources include meat, seafood, and Brazil nuts.

Understanding the importance of these vitamins and minerals allows for intentional dietary choices to ensure optimal nutritional intake on the ketogenic journey. It's essential to prioritize a diverse and nutrient-dense diet while considering individual needs and potential supplementation under the guidance of healthcare professionals.

Common Supplements for Women: Enhancing Wellness on the Ketogenic Journey

In this section, we explore common supplements that are particularly relevant for women following a ketogenic lifestyle. Understanding the unique nutritional needs of women allows for targeted supplementation to support overall health and well-being.

1. Omega-3 Fatty Acids:

Insight:

- Supports heart health, reduces inflammation, and may benefit hormonal balance.

- Found in fatty fish, flaxseeds, chia seeds, and fish oil supplements.

2. Calcium:

Insight:

- Essential for bone health, especially important for women.

- Sources include dairy, leafy greens, and calcium supplements if dietary intake is insufficient.

3. Iron:

Insight:

- Important for oxygen transport and preventing iron-deficiency anemia.

- Found in red meat, poultry, fish, and iron supplements if needed.

4. Vitamin D:

Insight:

- Crucial for bone health, immune function, and hormonal balance.

- Obtain from sunlight exposure, fatty fish, egg yolks, and vitamin D supplements if necessary.

5. Magnesium:

Insight:

- Supports muscle function, relaxation, and may alleviate menstrual symptoms.

- Found in nuts, seeds, leafy greens, and magnesium supplements if needed.

6. Folate (Vitamin B9):

Insight:

- Important for reproductive health, especially during pregnancy.

- Found in leafy greens, legumes, and folate supplements if necessary.

7. Vitamin B12:

Insight:

- Vital for energy metabolism and neurological health.

- Sources include meat, fish, eggs, and vitamin B12 supplements if needed, especially for those on a vegetarian or vegan diet.

8. Iron:

Insight:

- Important for women, especially during menstruation and pregnancy.

- Sources include red meat, poultry, fish, and iron supplements if needed.

9. Collagen:

Insight:

- Supports skin elasticity, joint health, and connective tissue.

- Found in bone broth, collagen supplements, and collagen-rich foods.

10. Probiotics:

Insight:

- Supports gut health, which is linked to overall well-being.

- Found in fermented foods and probiotic supplements.

11. Evening Primrose Oil:

Insight:

- May help alleviate symptoms of premenstrual syndrome (PMS).

- Contains gamma-linolenic acid (GLA), an omega-6 fatty acid.

12. Biotin:

Insight:

- Supports hair, skin, and nail health.

- Found in eggs, nuts, and biotin supplements if necessary.

13. Vitamin E:

Insight:

- Acts as an antioxidant, supporting skin health.

- Found in nuts, seeds, and vitamin E supplements.

14. Cranberry Extract:

Insight:

- May promote urinary tract health, particularly beneficial for women.

- Available as cranberry extract supplements.

Building a Supportive Community: Thriving Together on the Ketogenic Journey

In this section, we explore the importance of building a supportive community for individuals on the ketogenic journey. Creating connections with like-minded individuals provides encouragement, motivation, and a shared space for learning and growth.

1. Shared Experiences:

Insight:

- Connect with others who are on a similar ketogenic journey.

- Shared experiences create a sense of understanding and camaraderie.

2. Online Communities:

Insight:

- Join online ketogenic communities and forums.

- Platforms such as social media groups or dedicated forums provide opportunities to ask questions, share successes, and seek advice.

3. Local Meetups:

Insight:

- Explore local ketogenic meetups or events.

- Connecting with people in your area allows for face-to-face interactions and potential friendships.

4. Accountability Partners:

Insight:

- Partner with someone for mutual accountability.

- Having a friend or family member on the same journey enhances motivation and commitment.

5. Recipe Sharing:

Insight:

- Exchange ketogenic recipes and meal ideas.

- A supportive community can be a valuable source of culinary inspiration.

6. Fitness Challenges:

Insight:

- Participate in fitness challenges together.

- Encouraging each other in physical activities enhances motivation and fosters a sense of accomplishment.

7. Emotional Support:

Insight:

- Share your challenges and victories.

- A supportive community provides emotional support during both highs and lows.

8. Educational Resources:

Insight:

- Share educational articles, videos, or books related to the ketogenic lifestyle.

- Enhance collective knowledge and understanding of the principles behind the diet.

9. Group Learning Sessions:

Insight:

- Organize group learning sessions or workshops.

- Collaborative learning fosters a sense of community and shared growth.

10. Celebrate Milestones:

Insight:

- Celebrate individual and group milestones.

- Acknowledging achievements, whether big or small, reinforces a positive and encouraging atmosphere.

11. Non-Judgmental Environment:

Insight:

- Foster a non-judgmental and inclusive environment.

- A supportive community is built on understanding and acceptance of diverse experiences and goals.

12. Expert Guest Speakers:

Insight:

- Invite guest speakers or experts for virtual or in-person talks.

- Learning from professionals adds value and depth to the community's knowledge base.

13. Empowerment and Positivity:

Insight:

- Encourage empowerment and positivity.

- Focus on personal growth, well-being, and the positive aspects of the ketogenic lifestyle.

14. Adaptability to Individual Journeys:

Insight:

- Recognize and celebrate the diversity of individual journeys.

- A supportive community embraces different goals, preferences, and paths within the ketogenic lifestyle.

Online and Offline Support Groups: Nurturing Connection on the Ketogenic Path

In this section, we explore the benefits and strategies of both online and offline support groups for individuals on the ketogenic journey. Whether connecting virtually or in-person, these groups offer valuable support, encouragement, and shared experiences.

1. Online Support Groups:

Insight:

- Join online ketogenic communities on platforms like social media or dedicated forums.

- Benefit from a global network of individuals sharing insights, recipes, and motivation.

2. Virtual Meetups:

Insight:

- Participate in virtual meetups through video calls or webinars.

- Connect with like-minded individuals regardless of geographical location.

3. Facebook Groups:

Insight:

- Explore ketogenic Facebook groups.

- Engage in discussions, ask questions, and share experiences with a diverse online community.

4. Instagram Communities:

Insight:

- Connect with the ketogenic community on Instagram.

- Follow accounts, participate in challenges, and share your journey through posts and stories.

5. Dedicated Forums:

Insight:

- Join dedicated ketogenic forums.

- Platforms like Reddit offer specialized communities where you can find support and information.

6. Local Meetups:

Insight:

- Search for local ketogenic meetups or events.

- Meet fellow enthusiasts in your area for in-person connections.

7. Community Websites:

Insight:

- Explore community websites focused on ketogenic living.

- Access resources, forums, and events tailored to the ketogenic lifestyle.

8. In-Person Support Groups:

Insight:

- Attend local in-person ketogenic support groups.

- Share experiences, ask questions, and build connections with individuals in your community.

9. Fitness Classes or Groups:

Insight:

- Join fitness classes or groups with a ketogenic focus.

- Combine physical activity with social connections for a holistic approach to health.

10. Book Clubs:

Insight:

- Form or join ketogenic book clubs.

- Discuss literature related to the ketogenic lifestyle and build connections through shared reading.

11. Cooking Classes:

Insight:

- Attend ketogenic cooking classes or workshops.

- Learn new recipes and cooking techniques while connecting with others who share your dietary preferences.

12. Wellness Events:

Insight:

- Participate in wellness events or expos.

- Connect with vendors, experts, and individuals who share an interest in the ketogenic lifestyle.

13. Networking Events:

Insight:

- Attend networking events focused on health and wellness.

- Build connections with professionals and enthusiasts in the ketogenic space.

14. Workshops and Seminars:

Insight:

- Join workshops and seminars on ketogenic living.

- Learn from experts, ask questions, and connect with attendees who share similar goals.

Partner and Family Involvement: Fostering Ketogenic Support Together

In this section, we explore the significance of partner and family involvement in the ketogenic journey. Engaging loved ones in the process can enhance support, and understanding, and create a positive environment for sustainable success.

1. Open Communication:

Insight:

- Foster open communication with your partner and family.

- Share your goals, reasons for following a ketogenic lifestyle, and how their support can make a positive impact.

2. Education and Information:

Insight:

- Provide educational resources about the ketogenic lifestyle.

- Share articles, books, or videos that explain the principles and benefits of keto to enhance understanding.

3. Cooking Together:

Insight:

- Involve your partner and family in meal preparation.

- Cook together, experiment with ketogenic recipes, and make it a shared experience.

4. Family-Friendly Meals:

Insight:

- Adapt ketogenic meals to be family-friendly.

- Create variations that cater to different preferences while maintaining the core principles of the diet.

5. Joint Fitness Activities:

Insight:

- Engage in joint fitness activities.

- Whether it's walking, cycling, or attending fitness classes together, make physical activity a shared endeavor.

6. Goal Setting as a Family:

Insight:

- Set health and wellness goals as a family.

- Encourage each member to establish their objectives, fostering a supportive and motivating environment.

7. Celebrate Milestones Together:

Insight:

- Celebrate individual and collective milestones.

● Acknowledge achievements and progress, reinforcing the positive impact of the ketogenic journey.

8. Create a Supportive Environment:

Insight:

● Foster a supportive and understanding environment.

● Recognize that everyone may have different dietary preferences, and find common ground that accommodates both ketogenic and non-ketogenic choices.

9. Encourage Questions and Discussion:

Insight:

● Encourage your partner and family to ask questions.

● Address concerns, provide explanations, and involve them in decision-making processes related to the ketogenic lifestyle.

10. Meal Planning Together:

Insight:

● Collaborate on meal planning.

● Involve your partner and family in creating weekly menus that align with ketogenic principles while accommodating diverse tastes.

11. Mindful Eating Practices:

Insight:

● Introduce mindful eating practices to the family.

● Encourage awareness of food choices, portion sizes, and the enjoyment of meals together.

12. Emotional Support:

Insight:

● Seek emotional support from your partner and family.

● Share your challenges and successes, fostering a sense of connection and understanding.

13. Inclusivity in Social Gatherings:

Insight:

● Foster inclusivity during social gatherings.

- Find ways to incorporate ketogenic options into family events, making it easier to adhere to your dietary goals.

14. Flexibility and Understanding:

Insight:

- Be flexible and understanding of individual preferences.

- Find a balance that allows everyone to feel supported and respected in their dietary choices.

Maintaining a Ketogenic Lifestyle Long-Term: Sustainable Strategies for Success

In this section, we explore sustainable strategies for maintaining a ketogenic lifestyle over the long term. Establishing habits, addressing challenges, and adapting to evolving needs are essential aspects of a successful and enduring ketogenic journey.

1. Establishing Sustainable Habits:

Insight:

- Focus on building sustainable habits rather than short-term fixes.

- Gradual changes and consistency contribute to long-term success.

2. Diverse and Enjoyable Meals:

Insight:

- Explore diverse and enjoyable ketogenic meals.

- Keep the diet interesting by trying new recipes and incorporating a variety of flavors and ingredients.

3. Listen to Your Body:

Insight:

- Pay attention to your body's signals and needs.

- Adjust your ketogenic approach based on energy levels, hunger cues, and overall well-being.

4. Regular Health Checkups:

Insight:

- Schedule regular health checkups.

- Monitor key health markers and consult with healthcare professionals to ensure the ketogenic lifestyle aligns with your individual needs.

5. Flexibility and Adaptability:

Insight:

- Embrace flexibility and adaptability.

- Life circumstances and preferences may change; be open to adjusting your ketogenic approach accordingly.

6. Periodic Reassessments:

Insight:

- Periodically reassess your goals and motivations.

- Confirm that your ketogenic lifestyle aligns with your evolving health objectives and overall well-being.

7. Mindful Eating Practices:

Insight:

- Practice mindful eating.

- Be present during meals, savor flavors, and pay attention to hunger and fullness cues.

8. Social and Cultural Considerations:

Insight:

- Navigate social and cultural situations with flexibility.

- Find ways to enjoy social gatherings while adhering to your ketogenic principles.

9. Educate and Involve Others:

Insight:

- Educate and involve friends and family.

- Share information about your ketogenic lifestyle to foster understanding and support.

10. Celebrate Non-Scale Victories:

Insight:

- Celebrate non-scale victories.

- Recognize and appreciate the positive changes in energy levels, mental clarity, and overall well-being.

11. Experiment with Intermittent Fasting:

Insight:

- Consider experimenting with intermittent fasting.

- Incorporate fasting periods that align with your preferences and lifestyle.

12. Address Emotional Eating:

Insight:

- Address emotional eating triggers.

- Develop alternative coping mechanisms to manage emotions without turning to food.

13. Regular Physical Activity:

Insight:

- Prioritize regular physical activity.

- Choose activities you enjoy to make exercise a sustainable and enjoyable part of your routine.

14. Find a Supportive Community:

Insight:

- Maintain connections with a supportive community.

- Engage with individuals who share similar goals, providing encouragement and understanding.

Sustainability and Longevity: Nurturing a Lifelong Ketogenic Lifestyle

In this section, we delve into the principles of sustainability and longevity within the context of a ketogenic lifestyle. By adopting mindful practices and holistic approaches, you can nurture a lifelong commitment to health and well-being.

1. Holistic Well-Being:

Insight:

- Prioritize holistic well-being beyond dietary choices.

- Consider aspects such as mental health, stress management, and adequate sleep for overall vitality.

2. Mindful Food Choices:

Insight:

- Make mindful and informed food choices.

- Focus on nutrient-dense options, emphasizing the quality of ingredients in your ketogenic meals.

3. Intuitive Eating:

Insight:

- Embrace intuitive eating.

- Listen to your body's signals, recognizing hunger and fullness cues to guide your eating habits.

4. Whole Foods Emphasis:

Insight:

- Emphasize whole foods in your ketogenic diet.

- Prioritize fresh, minimally processed ingredients to maximize nutritional benefits.

5. Sustainable Practices:

Insight:

- Adopt sustainable practices in your ketogenic journey.

- Consider the environmental impact of your food choices and explore eco-friendly options.

6. Regular Physical Activity:

Insight:

- Maintain regular physical activity.

- Choose activities you enjoy, making exercise a sustainable and integral part of your lifestyle.

7. Stress Management:

Insight:

- Prioritize stress management techniques.

- Incorporate practices such as meditation, deep breathing, or yoga to promote overall well-being.

8. Quality Sleep:

Insight:

- Ensure quality sleep.

- Prioritize sufficient and restful sleep to support physical and mental health.

9. Periodic Assessments:

Insight:

- Conduct periodic assessments of your health and goals.

- Adjust your ketogenic approach based on changes in lifestyle, preferences, or health status.

10. Goal Refinement:

Insight:

- Refine your health and wellness goals.

- Regularly reassess and adjust your objectives to align with your evolving priorities.

11. Lifelong Learning:

Insight:

- Cultivate a mindset of lifelong learning.

- Stay informed about new developments in ketogenic research and nutrition to refine your approach.

12. Positive Mindset:

Insight:

- Foster a positive mindset.

- Approach your ketogenic journey with a sense of optimism, focusing on the benefits and successes.

13. Community Engagement:

Insight:

- Stay engaged with a supportive community.

- Connect with individuals who share similar values, providing encouragement and shared experiences.

14. Enjoy the Journey:

Insight:

- Enjoy the journey of self-discovery and growth.

- Celebrate the positive changes and experiences that come with your lifelong commitment to a ketogenic lifestyle.

Incorporating Flexibility into Ketogenic Lifestyle: Balancing Choices and Enjoyment

In this section, we explore the concept of incorporating flexibility into a ketogenic lifestyle. By finding a balance between adherence to principles and allowing room for choices, you can enhance enjoyment and sustainability in the long term.

1. Occasional Indulgences:

Insight:

- Allow for occasional indulgences.

- Incorporate treats or non-ketogenic foods in moderation to satisfy cravings and maintain a sense of balance.

2. Cyclical Ketogenic Approach:

Insight:

- Explore cyclical ketogenic approaches.

- Periods of higher carbohydrate intake, strategically planned, may offer flexibility without compromising overall progress.

3. Targeted Ketogenic Dieting:

Insight:

- Consider targeted ketogenic dieting.

- Introduce small amounts of carbohydrates around workouts to support exercise performance while maintaining ketosis.

4. Carb Cycling:

Insight:

- Experiment with carb cycling.

- Rotate days of higher and lower carbohydrate intake based on your preferences and activity levels.

5. Mindful Eating Out:

Insight:

- Practice mindful eating when dining out.

- Make informed choices at restaurants, focusing on ketogenic-friendly options while enjoying the social aspect of meals.

6. Social Occasions:

Insight:

- Navigate social occasions with flexibility.

- Find ways to enjoy gatherings while making choices that align with your ketogenic principles.

7. Travel Adaptability:

Insight:

- Be adaptable during travel.

- Plan ahead for ketogenic options but allow flexibility to enjoy local cuisines and experiences.

8. Learning from Experiences:

Insight:

- Learn from your experiences.

- Understand how your body responds to different levels of carbohydrate intake and adjust accordingly.

9. Embracing Variety:

Insight:

- Embrace dietary variety.

- Include a diverse range of ketogenic foods to enhance nutritional intake and enjoyment.

10. Personalized Approach:

Insight:

- Personalize your approach to flexibility.

- Tailor your ketogenic lifestyle to suit your individual preferences, goals, and tolerance for flexibility.

11. Experimentation and Observation:

Insight:

- Experiment and observe.

- Assess the impact of incorporating flexibility into your ketogenic lifestyle and make adjustments based on your observations.

12. Mindful Choices:

Insight:

- Make mindful choices.

- Be intentional about when and why you choose to incorporate flexibility, ensuring alignment with your overall well-being goals.

13. Periodic Assessments:

Insight:

- Conduct periodic assessments of your approach.

- Regularly evaluate the balance between adherence and flexibility to refine your strategy.

14. Joyful Eating:

Insight:

- Cultivate joyful eating experiences.

- Approach your ketogenic lifestyle with a positive mindset, allowing for moments of culinary delight and satisfaction.

Long-Term Health Considerations: Nurturing Wellness Beyond the Ketogenic Journey

In this section, we explore the long-term health considerations associated with a ketogenic lifestyle. By addressing key aspects of health maintenance, you can cultivate a well-rounded approach that supports overall well-being beyond the initial phases of the ketogenic journey.

1. Regular Health Checkups:

Insight:

- Schedule regular health checkups.

- Monitor key health markers, including blood lipids, glucose levels, and other relevant indicators, with the guidance of healthcare professionals.

2. Nutrient Diversity:

Insight:

- Emphasize nutrient diversity.

- Ensure a varied and nutrient-dense diet by incorporating a wide range of keto-friendly foods to meet your body's nutritional needs.

3. Micronutrient Supplementation:

Insight:

- Consider micronutrient supplementation.

- Based on individual requirements, discuss the potential need for supplements such as vitamins and minerals with healthcare professionals.

4. Hydration and Electrolytes:

Insight:

- Prioritize hydration and electrolyte balance.

- Maintain proper fluid intake and electrolyte levels to support overall health and well-being.

5. Gut Health Maintenance:

Insight:

- Focus on gut health maintenance.

- Include fermented foods, probiotics, and prebiotics in your diet to support a healthy gut microbiome.

6. Regular Physical Activity:

Insight:

- Maintain regular physical activity.

- Engage in activities you enjoy to promote cardiovascular health, muscular strength, and overall well-being.

7. Stress Management Techniques:

Insight:

- Incorporate stress management techniques.

- Practice mindfulness, meditation, or other stress-relief strategies to support mental and emotional health.

8. Sleep Quality:

Insight:

- Prioritize quality sleep.

- Establish consistent sleep patterns and create a conducive sleep environment for optimal rest.

9. Hormonal Health Awareness:

Insight:

- Be aware of hormonal health.

- Monitor hormonal balance, especially for women, and consult healthcare professionals if there are concerns.

10. Bone Health Considerations:

Insight:

- Address bone health considerations.

- Ensure sufficient intake of calcium, vitamin D, and other nutrients essential for bone health.

11. Mental and Emotional Well-Being:

Insight:

- Prioritize mental and emotional well-being.

- Cultivate positive relationships, seek support when needed, and foster a healthy mindset.

12. Periodic Goal Assessments:

Insight:

- Conduct periodic assessments of your health goals.

- Reevaluate and adjust your health objectives based on evolving needs and priorities.

13. Holistic Health Practices:

Insight:

- Embrace holistic health practices.

- Integrate complementary therapies or practices, such as acupuncture or massage, to support overall wellness.

14. Lifelong Learning:

Insight:

- Cultivate a mindset of lifelong learning.

- Stay informed about health-related developments and continue to expand your knowledge.

Adapting to Life Changes: Navigating Transitions in Your Ketogenic Journey

In this section, we explore strategies for adapting to life changes within the context of your ketogenic journey. By navigating transitions effectively, you can maintain a sustainable and resilient approach to ketosis.

1. Acknowledging Life Changes:

Insight:

- Acknowledge and accept life changes.

- Recognize that transitions are a natural part of life and may impact your daily routines and habits.

2. Flexibility in Routine:

Insight:

- Build flexibility into your routine.

- Create adaptable structures that can accommodate changes in schedules, responsibilities, or priorities.

3. Goal Reassessment:

Insight:

- Periodically reassess your goals.

- Life changes may warrant adjustments to your health and wellness objectives; be open to reevaluating and refining them.

4. Mindful Eating During Stress:

Insight:

- Practice mindful eating during stressful times.

- Be aware of emotional triggers that may impact dietary choices, and choose foods that align with your ketogenic principles.

5. Planning for Busy Periods:

Insight:

- Plan for busy periods.

- During hectic times, prioritize meal preparation, and have convenient keto-friendly options available to maintain dietary consistency.

6. Emotional Support Systems:

Insight:

- Cultivate emotional support systems.

- Lean on friends, family, or community members for support during life changes, fostering a sense of connection and understanding.

7. Flexibility in Exercise Routine:

Insight:

- Be flexible with your exercise routine.

- Modify workouts based on time constraints, location changes, or other factors, ensuring continued physical activity.

8. Reevaluating Social Dynamics:

Insight:

- Reevaluate social dynamics.

- Consider how life changes impact social interactions, and find ways to stay connected with supportive communities.

9. Prioritizing Self-Care:

Insight:

- Prioritize self-care during transitions.

- Ensure that your well-being remains a priority by incorporating self-care practices into your routine.

10. Identifying Triggers and Solutions:

Insight:

- Identify triggers and solutions.

- Recognize potential challenges associated with life changes and proactively develop strategies to address them.

11. Seeking Professional Guidance:

Insight:

- Seek professional guidance if needed.

- During significant life changes, consider consulting with healthcare professionals or wellness experts to adapt your ketogenic approach accordingly.

12. Embracing Change as Growth:

Insight:

- Embrace change as an opportunity for growth.

- View life changes as a chance to reassess, learn, and evolve within the context of your ketogenic journey.

13. Celebrating Adaptability:

Insight:

- Celebrate your adaptability.

- Recognize and celebrate your ability to navigate transitions while maintaining a commitment to your ketogenic lifestyle.

14. Creating a Supportive Environment:

Insight:

- Foster a supportive environment.

- Surround yourself with individuals who understand and respect your journey, providing encouragement during life changes.

Ketogenic Living Through Different Life Stages: Tailoring Your Approach for Optimal Well-Being

In this section, we explore how to tailor your ketogenic approach to different life stages. By recognizing the unique considerations and priorities at each stage, you can optimize your ketogenic lifestyle for sustainable well-being.

1. Ketogenic Living for Young Adults:

Insight:

- Prioritize nutrient-dense foods.

- Young adults can benefit from focusing on nutrient-rich ketogenic options to support growth, energy levels, and overall well-being.

2. Ketosis During Pregnancy:

Insight:

- Consult with healthcare professionals.

- If considering ketogenic living during pregnancy, seek guidance from healthcare providers to ensure nutritional adequacy and safety for both mother and baby.

3. Postpartum Adaptations:

Insight:

- Gradual reintroduction of ketosis.

- Postpartum, consider a gradual reintroduction of ketosis, with a focus on nutrient-dense foods to support recovery and energy levels.

4. Ketogenic Living for Families:

Insight:

- Family-friendly keto meals.

- Create family-friendly ketogenic meals with a variety of options to accommodate diverse preferences while maintaining the principles of the diet.

5. Ketogenic Lifestyle for Adolescents:

Insight:

- Educate and involve adolescents.

- Engage adolescents in the decision-making process, providing education and involving them in meal planning to foster a positive relationship with ketogenic living.

6. Ketogenic Approach for Midlife:

Insight:

- Focus on hormonal balance.

- Consider the impact of hormonal changes during midlife, emphasizing ketogenic choices that support hormonal balance and overall health.

7. Ketogenic Living for Seniors:

Insight:

- Address nutrient needs for seniors.

- Adapt ketogenic choices to address changing nutrient needs and potential considerations for bone health and muscle preservation in seniors.

8. Ketosis and Athletic Performance:

Insight:

- Adjust macronutrient ratios for athletes.

- Athletes may need to adjust macronutrient ratios to support energy demands while maintaining ketosis. Experimentation and professional guidance can be beneficial.

9. Ketogenic Approach for Stressful Periods:

Insight:

- Focus on stress management.

- During stressful periods, prioritize stress management techniques and mindful eating to support overall well-being.

10. Ketosis and Chronic Conditions:

Insight:

- Consult with healthcare professionals.

- Individuals with chronic conditions should consult healthcare professionals to tailor a ketogenic approach that aligns with their specific health needs.

11. Customizing for Dietary Preferences:

Insight:

- Customize for dietary preferences.

- Adapt your ketogenic approach to align with personal dietary preferences, ensuring a sustainable and enjoyable experience.

12. Ketogenic Living for Mental Health:

Insight:

- Consider mental health aspects.

- Acknowledge the potential impact of ketogenic living on mental health and seek a balanced approach that supports both physical and mental well-being.

13. Integrating Ketosis with Intermittent Fasting:

Insight:

- Combine with intermittent fasting mindfully.

● If incorporating intermittent fasting, do so mindfully, considering individual tolerance and health goals.

14. Lifelong Learning and Adaptation:

Insight:

● Embrace lifelong learning and adaptation.

● Continuously educate yourself about ketogenic living and be open to adapting your approach based on changing life stages, priorities, and health considerations.

Handling Social Situations and Special Occasions: Navigating Ketogenic Choices with Grace

In this section, we explore strategies for navigating social situations and special occasions while adhering to your ketogenic lifestyle. By approaching these events with mindfulness and preparation, you can enjoy social interactions while staying true to your dietary choices.

1. Communicating Dietary Choices:

Insight:

● Communicate your dietary choices.

● Politely inform hosts or friends about your ketogenic lifestyle in advance, allowing for understanding and potential accommodations.

2. Pre-Eating Strategically:

Insight:

● Eat before social events.

● Pre-eating can help curb hunger, making it easier to resist non-ketogenic temptations during social gatherings.

3. Bringing Keto-Friendly Dishes:

Insight:

● Contribute keto-friendly dishes.

● Bring a dish or snack that aligns with your ketogenic lifestyle to share with others and ensure you have suitable options.

4. Choosing Wisely from Menus:

Insight:

- Choose wisely from menus.

- Scan restaurant menus in advance and identify keto-friendly options to make informed choices when dining out.

5. Managing Alcohol Intake:

Insight:

- Be mindful of alcohol intake.

- If consuming alcohol, opt for low-carb options, and moderate your intake to stay within your dietary goals.

6. Focusing on Social Connections:

Insight:

- Emphasize social connections.

- Shift the focus from food to the enjoyment of social interactions, allowing the experience to be about connections rather than specific dishes.

7. Handling Questions with Grace:

Insight:

- Handle questions with grace.

- Respond confidently and positively to inquiries about your dietary choices, emphasizing the benefits and personal preferences that guide your decisions.

8. Preparing for Buffet-Style Events:

Insight:

- Strategize for buffet-style events.

- Survey the options, focus on keto-friendly choices, and avoid mindless grazing at buffet-style gatherings.

9. Practicing Mindful Eating:

Insight:

- Practice mindful eating.

- Savor each bite, eat slowly, and pay attention to hunger and fullness cues, allowing for a more intentional dining experience.

10. Enjoying Dessert Alternatives:

Insight:

- Enjoy keto-friendly dessert alternatives.

- Explore or prepare low-carb dessert options to indulge in a sweet treat without compromising your ketogenic lifestyle.

11. Having a Supportive Buddy:

Insight:

- Bring a supportive buddy.

- Attend social events with someone who understands and supports your dietary choices, providing encouragement and camaraderie.

12. Choosing Non-Food-Centric Activities:

Insight:

- Opt for non-food-centric activities.

- Suggest social activities that don't revolve around meals, such as outdoor excursions, games, or cultural events.

13. Staying Hydrated:

Insight:

- Stay hydrated.

- Keep water or other keto-friendly beverages on hand to stay hydrated and reduce the temptation to snack.

14. Having a Plan for Special Occasions:

Insight:

- Plan for special occasions.

- Anticipate upcoming events, plan your approach, and make conscious choices to align with your ketogenic goals.

Appendix: Resources and Additional Information

In this comprehensive appendix, you'll find a curated list of resources and additional information to enhance your understanding and implementation of the ketogenic lifestyle. These resources cover a wide range of topics, providing valuable insights, recipes, and tools to support your journey.

1. Books:

- "The Ketogenic Bible" by Jacob Wilson and Ryan Lowery

- "Keto Clarity: Your Definitive Guide to the Benefits of a Low-Carb, High-Fat Diet" by Jimmy Moore and Eric C. Westman

- "The Art and Science of Low Carbohydrate Living" by Jeff S. Volek and Stephen D. Phinney

- "The Keto Reset Diet: Reboot Your Metabolism in 21 Days and Burn Fat Forever" by Mark Sisson

2. Websites and Blogs:

- Diet Doctor[1]

- Perfect Keto

- Keto Connect[2]

- Ruled.Me[3]

3. Mobile Apps:

- MyFitnessPal: Track your daily food intake and macros.

- Carb Manager: Monitor your carb intake and access keto-friendly recipes.

- Cronometer: Log your meals and track nutritional values for a comprehensive view of your diet.

4. Online Communities:

- Reddit - r/keto: Engage with a supportive community, share experiences, and seek advice.

- Keto Forums on Bodybuilding.com: Connect with individuals following ketogenic lifestyles with a focus on fitness.

5. Recipe Websites:

- All Day I Dream About Food[4]

- KetoDiet App

- Wholesome Yum[5]

---

1. https://www.dietdoctor.com/

2. https://www.ketoconnect.net/

3. https://www.ruled.me/

4. https://alldayidreamaboutfood.com/

5. https://www.wholesomeyum.com/

6. Podcasts:

- The Keto Diet Podcast: Hosted by Leanne Vogel, covering various aspects of the ketogenic lifestyle.

- Keto For Normies: A podcast by Keto Connect, discussing practical tips and experiences with keto.

7. Scientific Research and Journals:

- PubMed: Access scientific articles and studies related to ketogenic diets and their effects on health.

8. Ketogenic Challenges and Events:

- 30-Day Keto Challenge: Join a 30-day challenge to kickstart your ketogenic journey.

9. Ketogenic Coaching and Consultation:

- Consider seeking guidance from certified ketogenic coaches or nutritionists for personalized support on your journey.

10. Tracking Tools:

- Use tools likeMyFitnessPal[6] orCronometer[7] to track your food intake, macros, and micronutrients.

---

6. https://www.myfitnesspal.com/

7. https://cronometer.com/

Glossary of Terms

This glossary provides definitions for key terms frequently used in the context of the ketogenic lifestyle.

1. Ketogenic Diet:

   - *Definition:* A high-fat, low-carbohydrate diet designed to induce a state of ketosis, where the body burns fat for fuel instead of carbohydrates.

2. Ketosis:

   - *Definition:* A metabolic state in which the body relies on ketones as a primary source of energy, typically achieved through carbohydrate restriction.

3. Ketones:

   - *Definition:* Molecules produced by the liver during the breakdown of fats, serving as an alternative energy source when glucose availability is limited.

4. Macros (Macronutrients):

   - *Definition:* Essential nutrients required in relatively large amounts for optimal health, including carbohydrates, proteins, and fats.

5. Net Carbs:

   - *Definition:* Total carbohydrates minus fiber and sugar alcohols, representing the amount of carbohydrates that impact blood sugar levels.

6. Fat Adaptation:

   - *Definition:* The process by which the body becomes efficient at utilizing fat for energy, often experienced during the transition to a ketogenic diet.

7. Insulin Resistance:

   - *Definition:* A condition in which cells fail to respond properly to insulin, leading to elevated blood sugar levels and increased insulin production.

8. Gluconeogenesis:

   - *Definition:* The metabolic process by which the body generates glucose from non-carbohydrate sources, such as proteins and fats.

9. Electrolytes:

- *Definition:* Minerals with an electric charge, including sodium, potassium, and magnesium, are crucial for maintaining fluid balance and supporting various bodily functions.

10. Intermittent Fasting:

- *Definition:* A dietary approach involving cycles of eating and fasting, with periods of restricted eating followed by periods of normal or increased food intake.

11. Metabolic Syndrome:

- *Definition:* A cluster of conditions, including abdominal obesity, insulin resistance, high blood pressure, and abnormal lipid levels, that increase the risk of cardiovascular diseases and type 2 diabetes.

12. Hormonal Balance:

- *Definition:* The equilibrium of hormones in the body, crucial for maintaining optimal health and various physiological functions.

13. Nutrient Density:

- *Definition:* The concentration of essential nutrients per calorie in a food item, emphasizing the nutritional quality of a diet.

14. Micronutrients:

- *Definition:* Essential vitamins and minerals are required in smaller quantities for proper physiological functioning.

15. Polyunsaturated Fats (PUFAs):

- *Definition:* Fats with multiple double bonds in their chemical structure, including omega-3 and omega-6 fatty acids, are considered beneficial for heart health.

16. Monounsaturated Fats (MUFAs):

- *Definition:* Fats with a single double bond in their chemical structure, found in foods like avocados and olive oil, are associated with heart health.

17. Saturated Fats:

- *Definition:* Fats with no double bonds in their chemical structure, commonly found in animal products and some plant oils.

18. Ketogenic Ratio:

- *Definition:* The ratio of fats to combined proteins and carbohydrates in a ketogenic diet, often expressed as a percentage.

19. Macronutrient Ratios:

- *Definition:* The proportion of macronutrients—carbohydrates, proteins, and fats—in a diet, typically expressed as a percentage of total caloric intake.

Understanding Nutrition Labels

Nutrition labels on food packaging provide valuable information about the nutritional content of a product. Here's a guide to help you interpret and understand the key components of nutrition labels:

1. Serving Size:

- *Definition:* Indicates the recommended serving size for the product.

- *Importance:* Helps you understand the quantity of nutrients listed in relation to a standard serving.

2. Calories:

- *Definition:* The total number of calories in one serving of the product.

- *Importance:* Helps you manage your calorie intake based on your dietary goals.

3. Total Fat:

- *Definition:* The sum of all types of fat in one serving, including saturated and trans fats.

- *Importance:* Aids in monitoring fat intake, especially for those following a ketogenic diet.

4. Saturated Fat:

- *Definition:* The amount of saturated fat in one serving.

- *Importance:* High intake of saturated fats may impact heart health, so it's essential to monitor and limit.

5. Trans Fat:

- *Definition:* Indicates the amount of trans fats in one serving.

- *Importance:* Trans fats can be harmful and are best minimized in the diet.

6. Cholesterol:

- *Definition:* The quantity of cholesterol in one serving.

- *Importance:* Monitoring cholesterol intake is important for cardiovascular health.

7. Sodium:

- *Definition:* The amount of sodium (salt) in one serving.

- *Importance:* Helps you manage sodium intake, crucial for those with high blood pressure or other health concerns.

8. Total Carbohydrates:

- *Definition:* The total amount of carbohydrates in one serving, including dietary fiber and sugars.

- *Importance:* Useful for those tracking carbohydrate intake, particularly on a ketogenic diet.

9. Dietary Fiber:

- *Definition:* The amount of dietary fiber in one serving.

- *Importance:* Dietary fiber is essential for digestive health and can help manage blood sugar levels.

10. Sugars:

- *Definition:* The quantity of added and natural sugars in one serving.

- *Importance:* Monitoring sugar intake is crucial for overall health, especially for those managing conditions like diabetes.

11. Protein:

- *Definition:* The amount of protein in one serving.

- *Importance:* Protein is essential for muscle maintenance and various bodily functions.

12. Vitamins and Minerals:

- *Definition:* Lists the percentage of daily recommended intake for certain vitamins and minerals.

- *Importance:* Helps you assess the nutritional value of the product and its contribution to your daily nutrient needs.

13. % Daily Value (%DV):

- *Definition:* Indicates the percentage of the daily recommended intake of each nutrient in one serving.

- *Importance:* Provides a quick overview of how much a serving contributes to your daily nutrient requirements.

14. Ingredients List:

- *Definition:* Enumerates the ingredients in the product, listed in descending order by weight.

- *Importance:* Helps you identify the components of the product and make informed choices based on dietary preferences or restrictions.

Additional Resources

Expand your knowledge and support your journey in ketogenic living with these additional resources:

Books:

- "The Art and Science of Low Carbohydrate Living" by Jeff S. Volek and Stephen D. Phinney

- "Keto Clarity: Your Definitive Guide to the Benefits of a Low-Carb, High-Fat Diet" by Jimmy Moore and Eric C. Westman

- "The Ketogenic Bible" by Jacob Wilson and Ryan Lowery

Websites and Blogs:

- Diet Doctor[1]

- Perfect Keto Blog

- Ruled.Me[2]

Mobile Apps:

- MyFitnessPal[3]: Track your food intake and monitor macronutrient ratios.

- Carb Manager[4]: Log your meals and keep track of net carbs.

- Cronometer[5]: Track your food intake and monitor micronutrient levels.

Online Communities:

- Reddit - r/keto: Engage with a supportive community, share experiences, and seek advice.

- Keto Forums on Bodybuilding.com: Connect with individuals following ketogenic lifestyles with a focus on fitness.

Recipe Websites:

- All Day I Dream About Food[6]: Explore a variety of keto-friendly recipes.

---

1. https://www.dietdoctor.com/

2. https://www.ruled.me/

3. https://www.myfitnesspal.com/

4. https://www.carbmanager.com/

5. https://cronometer.com/

6. https://alldayidreamaboutfood.com/

- KetoDiet App Blog: Find recipes and tips for a ketogenic lifestyle.

Podcasts:

- The Keto Diet Podcast: Hosted by Leanne Vogel, covering various aspects of the ketogenic lifestyle.

- Keto For Normies: A podcast by Keto Connect, discussing practical tips and experiences with keto.

Scientific Research and Journals:

- PubMed: Access scientific articles and studies related to ketogenic diets and their effects on health.

Ketogenic Challenges and Events:

- 30-Day Keto Challenge by Diet Doctor: Join a 30-day challenge to kickstart your ketogenic journey.

Ketogenic Coaching and Consultation:

- Consider seeking guidance from certified ketogenic coaches or nutritionists for personalized support on your journey.

Tracking Tools:

- Use tools likeMyFitnessPal[7] orCronometer[8] to track your food intake, macros, and micronutrients.

---

7. https://www.myfitnesspal.com/

8. https://cronometer.com/

Frequently Asked Questions (FAQs) about Ketogenic Living

Q1: What is a Ketogenic Diet?

- A: A ketogenic diet is a low-carbohydrate, high-fat diet designed to induce ketosis, a metabolic state where the body burns fat for energy. It typically involves reducing carb intake and increasing fat consumption.

Q2: How does Ketosis Work?

- A: When carb intake is low, the body produces ketones from fat breakdown. Ketones become the primary energy source, allowing the body to enter a state of ketosis.

Q3: What Foods are Allowed on a Ketogenic Diet?

- A: Foods rich in healthy fats, moderate in protein, and low in carbohydrates are recommended. Examples include meat, fish, eggs, dairy, nuts, seeds, and low-carb vegetables.

Q4: Can I Eat Fruits on a Ketogenic Diet?

- A: Fruits are generally limited due to their natural sugar content. Berries in moderation (e.g., strawberries, raspberries) are lower in carbs and can be included.

Q5: How Long does it Take to Reach Ketosis?

- A: It varies, but it typically takes 2-7 days of reducing carb intake for the body to enter ketosis. Factors like individual metabolism and activity level play a role.

Q6: What are the Benefits of a Ketogenic Diet?

- A: Benefits may include weight loss, improved mental clarity, increased energy levels, and better blood sugar control. It may also have therapeutic effects in certain medical conditions.

Q7: Can I Exercise on a Ketogenic Diet?

- A: Yes, exercise can be part of a ketogenic lifestyle. Some may experience an adjustment period, but many find improved endurance and performance.

Q8: How do I Track Macros on a Ketogenic Diet?

- A: Use apps like MyFitnessPal or Carb Manager to track your daily intake of macronutrients (carbs, fats, proteins). Adjust ratios based on your goals.

Q9: Is the Ketogenic Diet Safe?

- A: For most people, a well-formulated ketogenic diet is safe. However, those with certain health conditions (e.g., kidney issues) should consult with a healthcare professional.

Q10: How can I Overcome Keto Flu?

- A: Keto flu symptoms (fatigue, headaches) can be alleviated by staying hydrated, ensuring sufficient electrolyte intake, and gradually adapting to the diet.

Q11: Can I Follow a Ketogenic Diet if I'm Vegetarian or Vegan?

- A: Yes, a vegetarian or vegan ketogenic diet is possible. Focus on plant-based fats, proteins, and low-carb vegetables. Consult with a nutritionist for guidance.

Q12: How can I Maintain Ketosis While Dining Out?

- A: Choose keto-friendly options like grilled meats, salads, and vegetables. Ask for substitutions if needed, and be mindful of hidden sugars in sauces.

Q13: Can I Drink Alcohol on a Ketogenic Diet?

- A: Moderate consumption of low-carb alcoholic beverages (e.g., dry wine, spirits) is possible, but alcohol metabolism may temporarily pause ketone production.

Q14: How Long Should I Follow a Ketogenic Diet?

- A: The duration varies. Some follow it for short-term goals, while others adopt it as a long-term lifestyle. Regular health check-ups are advisable for long-term adherence.

Index

Is the Ketogenic Diet Safe?

How Can I Overcome Keto Flu?

Can I Follow a Ketogenic Diet if I'm Vegetarian or Vegan?

How can I Maintain Ketosis While Dining Out?

Can I Drink Alcohol on a Ketogenic Diet?

How Long Should I Follow a Ketogenic Diet?

N. Index

Comprehensive Index for Quick Reference

Disclaimer:

The information provided in this textbook on ketogenic living for women is intended for general informational purposes only. It is not a substitute for professional medical advice, diagnosis, or treatment. Always seek the advice of your physician or other qualified health provider with any questions you may have regarding a medical condition.

The authors and contributors to this textbook make no representations or warranties of any kind, express or implied, about the completeness, accuracy, reliability, suitability, or availability of the information provided. Any reliance you place on the information is strictly at your own risk.

The content in this textbook may not be suitable for everyone, and individual responses to dietary changes may vary. It is essential to consult with a healthcare professional before making significant changes to your diet, especially if you have pre-existing health conditions, are pregnant, or breastfeeding.

Don't miss out!

Visit the website below and you can sign up to receive emails whenever DNT Publishing publishes a new book. There's no charge and no obligation.

https://books2read.com/r/B-A-VPQCB-JIVVC

BOOKS 2 READ

Connecting independent readers to independent writers.